Your Home Is Money

By The Editors Of Consumer Guide®

With Jerry C. Davis

Your Home Is Money

Managing Your Home For Profit

McGraw-Hill Book Company

New York   St. Louis   San Francisco   Dusseldorf   Mexico   Toronto

Contents

Introduction 6

Homes represent one of the best investments available today to middle-income Americans. Here are some reasons why, and here are some ways that you can cash in on the financial bonanza in residential real estate.

Part I

Making Money On Your Home 10

While most owners think they have to sell in order to reap the profits in their homes, that is not always the case. Various methods of refinancing the property allow an owner to tap the otherwise wasted asset of value appreciation and equity without surrendering title or moving off the property. Renting, on the other hand, can prove highly profitable to owners who can afford to operate two residences simultaneously.

Refinancing 13
Rent For Profit 23
Profit By Selling 32

Louis Weber, President
Publications International, Ltd.
3841 West Oakton Street
Skokie, Illinois 60076

1 2 3 4 5 6 7 8 9 0 BABA 7 8 3 2 1 0 9 8 7

Library of Congress Cataloging in Publication Data:

Main entry under title:

Your home is money

  1. House buying   2. House selling
I. Consumer guide
HD1379.Y68   643   78-5811

ISBN: 0-07-018997-8
ISBN: 0-07-018998-6 (pbk)

Part II

Maintaining And Improving The Home For Profit 46

After buying, the profit-minded owner can do plenty to maintain or increase property value. But there are pitfalls to be avoided when it comes to modernizing and adding to the home—pitfalls that can destroy profits.

Modernizing And Adding To The Home 50
Controlling Heating And Cooling Costs 55

Part III

What Should You Buy? 62

The eventual profitability of a home depends on the type of property it is, its location, and the investor's ability to evaluate real estate trends.

Single-Family Homes Vs. Other Types Of Investment Property 66
Building Vs. Buying Standing Property 70
What Can You Afford? 74
Where You Should Buy 77

The Process Of Buying 80

The financial aspects of purchasing a home can be confusing, but they are crucial in determining the ultimate value of the investment. Here are some ways to understand the process of buying and to use professional real estate people—brokers, lenders, agents—to best advantage.

Selecting The Residence 83
Negotiating For The Home 93
Arranging Financing 100
Closing The Deal 106
Insuring The New Home 110
Paying Real Estate Taxes 115

Appendices 118

Do-It-Yourself Property Appraising 118
Real Estate Record Keeping 122
Glossary Of Real Estate Terms 124
Principal And Interest Tables 132
Directory Of HUD And VA Regional Offices 154

Index 157

Introduction

THE AMERICAN home offers everything a good investment should — and much more! Consider these financial benefits of home ownership:

• Home values have risen at a rate greater than the rate of inflation for many years, meaning that a home has returned a profit in real dollars — not just inflated dollars — to its owner. Frequently, home appreciation figures have exceeded the rise in the cost of living by one or two percent, and recently homes have topped the annual increase in the consumer price index by a whopping three to four percent!

• A home is a great instrument for financial leverage. The home buyer puts only 20 percent of the value of the investment (sometimes less) into the property to realize 100 percent of its benefits. Compare that to leveraging in the stock market where buying securities on margin requires that the investor put up 70 percent or more of the value of the stock and then pay a higher rate of interest on the loan than the rate the typical homeowner pays on a mortgage.

• The risk a buyer assumes by investing in a home is minimal. True, some home values decline due to the property or the neighborhood or the community suffering from negligence or unusual economic circumstances. But the well-located home in a neighborhood where pride in ownership prevails, and in a city free from severe economic reversals, will increase in value during the best of times *and* the worst of times.

• Lenders respect the value of a home and are willing to assist with this kind of investment in a more generous manner than they are with any other type of borrowing. They offer interest rates on home mortgages that are lower than those on loans for investing in stocks or business ventures or other types of real estate. Lenders also recognize that home values appreciate over the years, and they allow owners to borrow against that increased value — again at attractive interest rates. Thus, the homeowner who knows how to refinance his or her property wisely can make money even without selling. Using a home for such profitable purposes will be a key consideration in this book.

• The federal government encourages home investment by offering special tax breaks and other incentives to purchasers of residential property. The best known tax advantage — the deduction for interest paid on mortgage loans and real estate taxes — actually amounts to homeowners receiving a subsidy from the government. But that's not all! The government also aids the investor by guaranteeing (through the Federal Housing Administration and Veterans Administration) home mortgage loans. Lenders, assured that their money is protected, will frequently allow buyers to borrow up to 95 percent of the value of a home — sometimes even 100 percent! For very few dollars of personal investment, therefore, the homeowner can control (and realize the benefits from) a substantial piece of wealth.

• The government's beneficence extends even to the day the owner realizes maximum profitability — i.e., when the home is sold. The return on the investment is taxed as a capital gain — not the straight income that is assessed with other types of windfall profits — and no tax at all is collected if the investor reinvests the profits back into a residence of the same or higher value that he or she will soon occupy.

• Local governments also help the home investor. For example, the assessor assigns a lower tax rate to housing than to commercial property. In addition, local governments often improve homeowners' property directly by adding sidewalks or gutters and indirectly by building recreational facilities or schools or highways nearby. Such construction can heighten home values enormously. In many instances, homeowners also get better service from their local government than renters receive. Local officials consider property owners to be permanent residents, deserving of more attention as tax-paying citizens than the supposedly transient renters.

The Best Investment

IT ALL adds up to the home standing supreme as an investment opportunity. But like any investment, of course, making a profit on a home depends on the demand.

Here, too, all the evidence points to the wisdom of home ownership. According to the federal government, fewer homes are being built than the demand for homes warrants. A 1969 study revealed that the nation needed to build

---

The home stands as the supreme investment opportunity for most middle-income Americans.

2.3 million new homes a year through 1980 to house the number of people seeking shelter. In only one year (1974) has that goal been met. In some years, only 1.2 million to 1.5 million new homes have been built, creating a severe supply-demand imbalance. One result of this imbalance has been a doubling of the five to six percent annual increase in the price of housing from the 1960's to the mid-1970's.

Even when in 1977 home builders came close to meeting national new housing goals, people who already owned homes profited. The approximately two million homes built during 1977 did little to dent the demand, but they did cause shortages of material, labor, and money that drove housing prices up sharply. People who owned homes built several years ago benefitted from these cost increases by being able to sell their homes at prices competititve with the new ones but significantly higher than what they had paid. Many existing homes rose in value from eight to 15 percent during the course of a year when homebuilding was near its all-time peak.

Some Do Better Than Others

WITHIN THIS rewarding market, where almost everybody who owns a home makes money, some investors make more money than others. The purpose of this book is to show how the smart homeowners maximize their profits and how you can do the same.

Part of this advice concerns timing. People who purchased homes in 1961, 1966, 1971, and perhaps in 1976 should be set for life in terms of shelter. Those were the vintage years of the housing market, and the people who bought then already have realized enough profit to upgrade their living standard a considerable degree.

Recall the characteristics of those years. There was great competition in the market as construction was booming and builders were keeping their prices down in order to remain competitive. Mortgage money was plentiful at comparatively low interest rates, and existing homeowners were taking advantage by re-financing to improve their present home or upgrading by acquiring a more valuable property. They had no problem selling and none buying.

Thus, timing a home purchase right is crucial to maximizing profitability. But knowing when to sell can be equally critical. Those investors who foresaw the tight money conditions and high interest rates of 1974-75 (there were clear signals) and sold before the credit crunch hit garnered the best profits available. The smartest ones of all bought more expensive property at the same time they sold, getting mortgages with lower interest rates than have been around for the last few years. As a consequence, these seller/buyers are now realizing the benefits of both a well-timed sale and the ownership of a more valuable asset that has increased and will continue to increase in profitability as the years pass.

Buying and selling are not the only ways to make a profit on a home investment, however. By refinancing or renting or exchanging the property, an investor can capture dollars that are not taxed, that don't require surrendering ownership, and that in some circumstances produce more profitable results than an outright sale would. Of course, maintaining and improving a personal residence can also lead to greater profits as well as a nicer home, but beware! Some improvements add value to property while others don't. The smart investor is always thinking of ways to make a splendid asset even more valuable while avoiding costly mistakes that don't pay off in the end.

Your Home Is Money

OWNING A HOME has long been one of the great satisfactions of life, but many homeowners have not yet realized that housing (especially during the final quarter of the 20th century) represents far more than a source of shelter. A home — your home — is money. Handled as carefully, prudently, and intelligently as any sizable investment should be, the home can return a level of profitability comparable with any financial opportunity available to most Americans.

Part I: Making

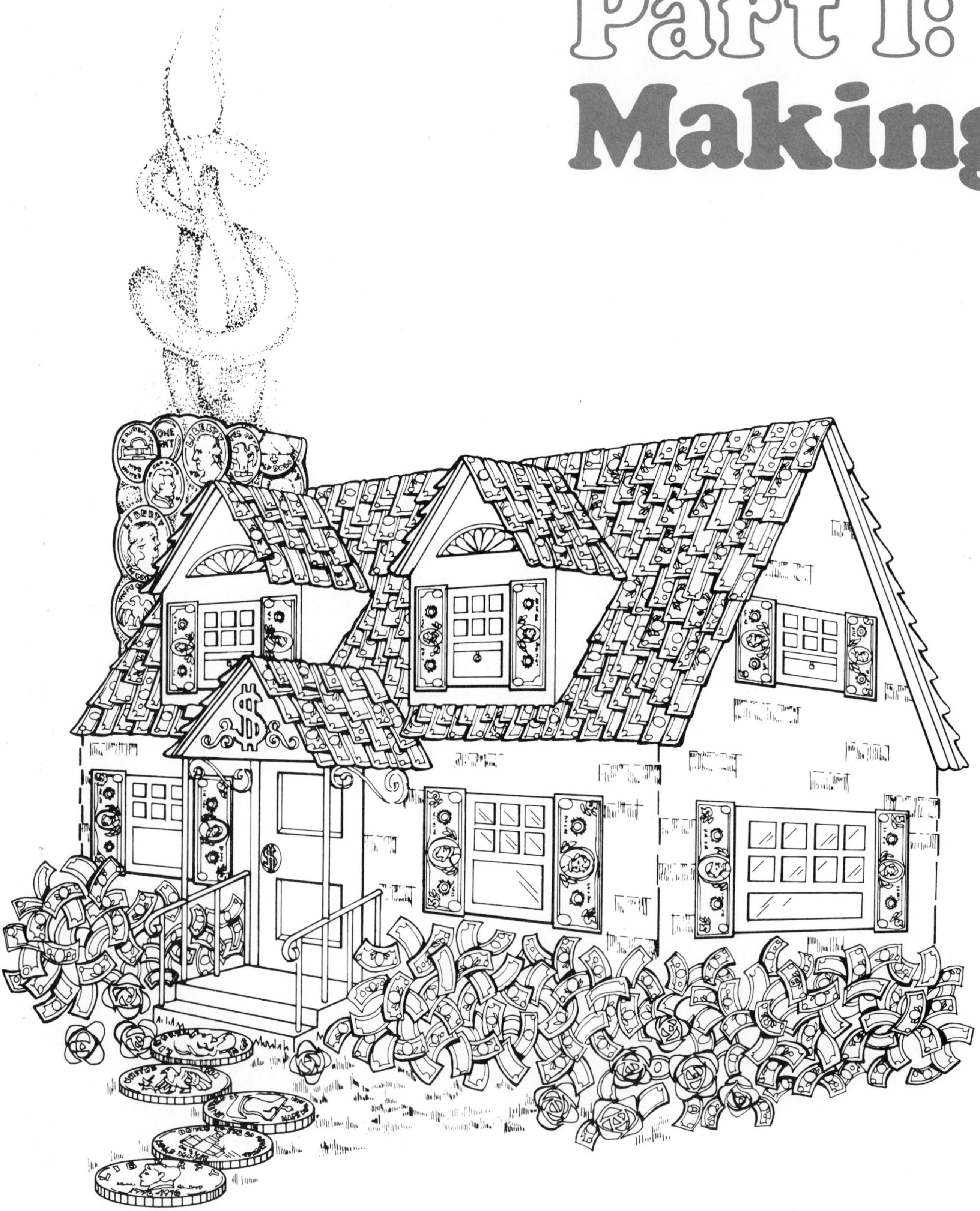

Money On Your Home

THE DAY that a homeowner realizes that his or her property has appreciated in value by 10 percent is the day he or she should begin thinking about how and when to reap the profit. That 10 percent appreciation figure assures the homeowner that selling the property will provide a sufficient return to cover both the expenses inherent in the selling process and the cost of moving to a new residence.

But selling isn't the only way to make money on residential real estate, as this section will demonstrate. Refinancing and renting represent other methods of extracting the potential profit in a home. The smart homeowner knows about these methods and seeks to put the home asset to work, making life more comfortable and affluent instead of letting the home's financial possibilities go unused and wasted.

For the last 25 years, the best place to invest money has been in real estate. Many home investors have seized upon the appreciation in real estate values to upgrade to more expensive homes, but other possibilities exist. For example, two homes might be better than one (especially if they are attached as in a two-flat or duplex), allowing the owner to live in one and rent out the other. In this way the owner gains in-come and tax shelter as well as a roof over his or her head. Furthermore, the appreciation of two units can mean twice the total profit available from a single unit.

The whole concept of a home investment should be to accumulate wealth. Sometimes that accumulation is a subtle process, as Chicago real estate appraiser Eugene Stunard points out: "The most likely property to show a profit for the small investor is something he purchases for his own use. From a strict dollars and cents standpoint, many investments today don't produce much cash return. But by purchasing a building to dwell or work in, an investor fixes his costs over the term of the mortgage. Thus, when inflation gallops ahead and everything else costs more, his investment will go up in value, too, because it cannot be duplicated or replaced for less." Stunard adds that many home investors "acquire a nestegg without any real knowledge of real estate."

Clearly, a home produced one year for $40,000 cannot be duplicated or replaced a year later for the same $40,000. Higher costs for labor, materials, land, and mortgage money might well push the price of that home to $44,000. Thus, double digit inflation may be bad news for the country,

Inflation
can be made
to serve the purposes
of home investors.

but as it pushes up the value of homes, it serves the purposes of homeowners who know how to make the most out of an investment in residential real estate.

Usually, in fact, homes appreciate at a faster rate than inflation, as homeowner Tom Gunsett found when he had his property appraised in 1976. During a period in which the Consumer Price Index had shown an increase of almost 80 percent, Gunsett's $30,000 home had shown about a gain in value of about 133 percent. Without selling his home — presently appraised at $70,000 — Gunsett was sitting on a $40,000 profit.

Gunsett knew exactly what he wanted to do with that $40,000 and with the $12,000 he had accumulated in equity over the years. Like most middle management employees, Gunsett had not been able to come even close to saving enough to finance his children's education. The son was two years away from college and the daughter four years when Gunsett decided to do something.

Refinancing looked very attractive. Even though Gunsett would have to surrender his 6 percent mortgage for an 8.5 percent loan, he would be doing much better than borrowing the funds for a college education at the going rate of 14 percent. In addition, the increased interest payments would mean a higher tax deduction, partially offsetting the disparity in monthly payments. For the relatively short period before the cash was actually needed to pay college expenses, Gunsett planned to put the proceeds of the refinancing into certificates of deposit.

Taking advantage of the refinancing option — in contrast to selling the home — meant no family disruption at a time when school activities and neighborhood friends were especially important to the Gunsett children. Better to sell later when both children were away at college and space requirements had changed so that a different type of living unit, more fitting to the family's needs, could be acquired.

Selling, moreover, would be expensive, involving $5,000 to $6,000 in closing and moving costs. The time-consuming process of finding a new home was another factor to be considered, and, besides, the family liked the house it was in.

Renting was not so attractive for the Gunsetts because they had not been able to accumulate enough savings to buy another house while keeping the one they had. They recognized that by renting they would have steady income and better tax deductions while paying off the rest of their low-interest mortgage, and they liked the thought of earning at least $200 a month over their mortgage payments in return on the property. But the Gunsetts needed much more capital than the $2,400 a year they would derive from renting.

So Tom Gunsett proceeded with the refinancing option and netted a total of $36,000. Perhaps that wouldn't cover college costs for both children, but it was cash that would have cost much more to acquire in any other way. And if the Gunsett property continued to appreciate in value, another refinancing might very well be in order in another five years.

Refinancing

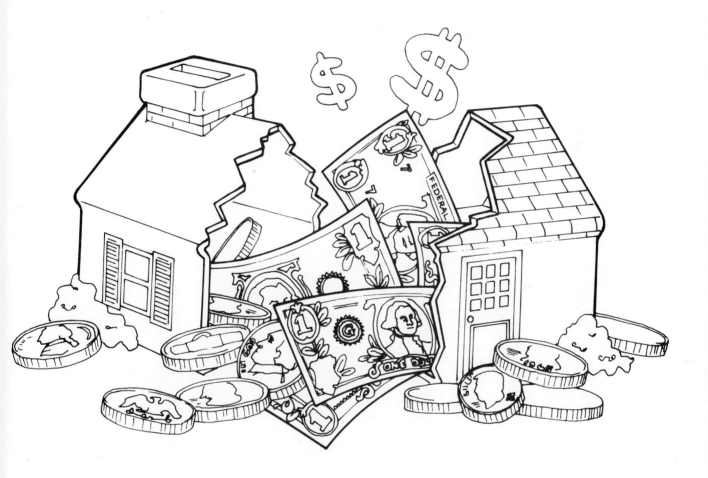

THE NICE THING about owning real estate is that you do not have to sell it in order to realize an often substantial amount of untaxed profit. That profit, curiously, remains untouched by many homeowners, prompting investment counselors to refer to it as a "wasted asset" because it brings its owner no monetary return.

The profit consists of the accumulated appreciation in value and buildup of equity in a home. To tap into it, to start putting that wasted asset to work, the homeowner simply has to borrow against some or all of the home's total current value — the process that is called refinancing.

Think about the possibilities refinancing provides. First, it allows the homeowner to capitalize on the profit that others have realized only by selling their homes. Of course there are often good reasons to sell, but selling a house requires finding another place to live, and that's when the homeowner quickly learns about an unpleasant aspect of the current home market. To buy a similar residence or a better one, one must pay an inflated price that cancels the inflation-fueled appreciation gained on the sale of the present home. It is one of the unavoidable costs one must pay for relocating.

Refinancing, on the other hand, enables the homeowner to stay put and receive the benefits of inflation rather than suffering its liabilities.

Second, refinancing puts in the homeowner's hands money that is free of taxes. The proceeds pulled out via refinancing are not subject to the capital gains tax that is imposed when a home is sold. The money received takes the form of a loan, and the government does not tax loans. In fact, the government allows a tax deduction on the interest costs of the loan.

When an owner sells a home, he or she must reinvest the profit gained on the home's appreciation in value in another residence within 18 months or else pay the capital gains tax; in contrast, refinancing not only puts tax-free dollars in the homeowner's hands to do with as he or she likes, but it also lowers his or her total tax liability. When the owner eventually sells a refinanced home, he or she must pay a tax on the higher value, but until that time the tax is deferred.

Third, refinancing saves the homeowner a substantial part of the fees that go with selling one property and buying another. For example, a broker ordinarily charges a six to seven percent real estate commission to sell a home. In typical refinancing the owner pays fees for a new title search, an appraisal, and legal counsel, and in some cases he or she might also have to pay "points," the one-time service charge (usually one or two percent of the mortgage value) that a lender requires for a new loan. But all these fees must also be paid by the person selling a home — in addition to that sizable broker's commission.

Fourth and finally, refinancing produces bigger income tax deductions because the homeowner will be making higher interest pay-

> Refinancing is an often overlooked technique for utilizing what investment counselors call the "wasted asset."

ments on the new and larger mortgage. Sometimes, the tax savings can almost make up the difference between the cost of one of those fine old low-interest loans and today's mortgages of 9.5 percent and up.

People living in the same home for 15 to 20 years are paying much more in equity than in interest on their mortgage. That means they have much less to deduct in federal and state income taxes. By taking out a new mortgage, amounting to perhaps as much as 80 percent of the appreciated value of the home, these people could restore their large interest deductions. Depending on one's tax bracket, a sizable deduction obtained through refinancing could result in a substantially reduced income tax.

For example, consider the person owning a $36,000 home purchased in 1962 with a $30,000 mortgage at six percent. After 15 years, the federal income tax deduction for interest on that loan has been reduced to approximately $1,250 a year. Now the owner refinances at 8.75 percent, taking a $50,000 mortgage on the home that has doubled in value so that it is now worth $72,000. The first-year tax deduction jumps from $1,250 to $4,200. A person in a 35 percent or higher tax bracket would probably find that the reduced amount of tax he or she must pay would almost offset the difference between a loan at six percent and one at 8.75 percent.

Lenders like this kind of transaction, too. They not only get a higher interest rate on the home mortgage, but they also satisfy the needs of a customer who may give them additional business with the proceeds of the refinancing.

The major drawback to refinancing, of course, is the steep increase in payments. For example, an old $30,000 mortgage at six percent interest may carry monthly principal and interest payments amounting to $199.50. A new $60,000 mortgage at 8.5 percent interest on the same home that has appreciated in value, however, can place a monthly burden in mortgage costs (principal and interest) amounting to $461.40.

People whose income has risen steadily during the years they have owned a home can usually handle a stiff increase in mortgage payments. Some of the increase, moreover, is offset by larger income tax deductions. But no one who is contemplating the refinancing of a home can afford to ignore the substantial jump in monthly payments that are part of the refinancing process.

Why Refinance?

REFINANCING a house should have some purpose beyond just putting money into a savings account. It makes no sense to take out a loan at 8.5 percent or more unless one can either get more than that in return on the funds obtained or else put those funds to some other worthy use.

Paying for a college education by refinancing real estate is one way to bring about an acceptable return. Educational loans usually carry a higher interest rate than home mortgages.

Therefore, parents would save the difference in interest payments by refinancing their home instead of taking out an educational loan for their college-bound child.

Some people consistently pay large monthly fees to retail stores or a bank credit card; these fees can run as high as 18 percent annually. By pulling some of the equity out of a house to pay off large bills and avoid those 18 percent charges, a homeowner is using refinancing in a highly profitable manner.

High-yield investments, ones that return more than the eight or nine percent mortgage rates that currently prevail, are not only available but represent an excellent way to reap dollars on the otherwise "wasted asset."

People who are currently paying a second mortgage may find it advantageous to refinance the first mortgage and pay off the very costly second mortgage. A second mortgage typically runs three percent above the rate of a first mortgage, and it must be paid back over a shorter term. Refinancing in this instance is almost certain to produce lower monthly payments.

Most people, however, refinance for one of two basic reasons. They either want to invest in a business that they believe will return capital at a higher rate than the interest they will be paying the mortgage lender, or they want to put the money into their own homes in the form of major improvements that will increase its value and add to its annual appreciation. An investment in the right kind of improvement is one of the best a homeowner can make because it increases the basic value of the home which is appreciating every year.

A $5,000 investment in a renovated kitchen and bath, for example, might add $8,000 to the overall value of the house, and that $8,000 will appreciate at the same rate as the house does. Assuming an average appreciation of eight percent for the entire house, the original $5,000 investment producing an $8,000 improvement will return $14,400 in five years. In addition, the homeowner will be able to deduct the interest paid on the original $5,000 loan from his or her income taxes.

Refinancing
a mortgage
frequently
benefits
both borrower
and lender.

The Basic Refinanced Mortgage

BASIC REFINANCING begins when an owner asks a financial institution to reappraise a home with an existing mortgage, and then to provide a new loan of up to 80 percent of the current value of the home. If the lender agrees to refinance, the original mortgage is then paid off and the homeowner receives in cash the difference between that pay-out and the new loan.

Here is the experience of a midwestern homeowner who recently went through a typical refinancing of his home. The owner had purchased the house in the early 1960's when a mortgage at a six percent interest rate was available. At that time, the lender appraised the property at $28,000 and granted an 80 percent mortgage ($22,400) on it. The buyer paid the other $5,600 as a downpayment.

Over the next 15 years, the house appreciated in value until in 1977 it was worth $50,000. During the same 15 years, the homeowner had reduced the original $22,400 mortgage principal down to $17,400, which meant that the homeowner had added $5,000 to his equity in the house. That, plus the $5,600 downpayment, plus the $22,000 appreciation in value of the property totaled a $32,600 asset.

While this asset was appreciating, the homeowner had found a small shopping center that he was certain would bring a good return; all the stores in it had leases with several years to run, and all were making money. With some initial capital the homeowner knew he could buy the center, earn 12 percent a year on his investment, and obtain the tax advantages of owning investment property. He would also reap the potential appreciation in the center's value.

The problem was that the homeowner did not have the $15,000 downpayment a financial institution required before granting a mortgage on the shopping center. His solution was to refinance his home and put some of that $32,600 "wasted asset" into the new investment.

The lender who held the homeowner's mortgage was delighted. The old loan at six percent interest could be crossed off the books and a new loan at a higher interest rate could be drafted.

Since the borrower did not have to refinance 80 percent of the value of the property to get the needed investment capital, he was able to get a better interest rate — 8.5 percent instead of the current 8.75 percent rate on an 80 percent loan. Lenders traditionally offer a lower rate when their risk is reduced by the extra cushion of a larger downpayment. Closing costs — including title search, appraisal, attorney's fees, and a one percent charge to obtain the loan — reduced the homeowner's net payoff, but he came out with more than enough to cover the $15,000 downpayment on his new investment.

Summing up his refinancing experience, the homeowner could point to several advantages and several disadvantages. First, the negatives: His interest rate went up 2.5 percent from the original mortgage, and his monthly principal and interest payments on the home increased from $134.40 to $269.15. In addition, he spent about $1,100 in various fees to obtain the loan; some of these fees, however, were tax deductible.

The positive aspects of refinancing, moreover, far outweighed the negatives. The homeowner invested in a property that returned 12 percent a year while paying only 8.5 percent for the money to make that investment. The tax deduction for interest on his personal residence increased from about $800 a year to approximately $3,000, and in his 30 percent tax bracket that saved the homeowner about $900 a year compared to the $240 saving he would have realized from continuing to pay interest on the original mortgage. In addition, he obtained tax deductions on the acquired shopping center which further reduced his total tax burden.

In this example, the borrower worked with the savings and loan association that held the original mortgage, but that is not necessarily the best way to refinance. Often it pays to shop around among several lenders because a lender other than the one who made the original mortgage may offer a substantially better deal on the refinanced mortgage. The homeowner, however, should be prepared to show a different lender cancelled checks to confirm that he or she has made mortgage payments on time;

Watch out for a prepayment penalty that could negate the profit in refinancing.

asking one's present lender for a verification of payment record is also a good idea. Either proof of financial reliability will ease the way toward refinancing with a new institution.

One factor that could upset refinancing plans is an original mortgage that specifies a prepayment penalty. Formerly, lenders frequently inserted a clause wherein prepayment of the loan by more than 20 percent a year carried a three percent penalty on the remaining principal. This clause is not common today; in fact, it cannot be applied to any loan with an interest rate of more than eight percent. Homeowners who find such a clause in their mortgages, however, must include the penalty in their calculations when deciding whether refinancing is a wise investment or not.

The Open-End Mortgage

REFINANCING BY taking out a new and larger mortgage and paying off the old one is by no means the only way to get equity out of a home. There is, for example, the open-end mortgage. Most mortgages are open-ended; that is, they allow the borrower to ask for what lenders call "additional advances." What this really means is that the amount of principal which the homeowner has already paid off can be added back to the mortgage; the homeowner can then receive that sum as a cash loan. In addition to accumulated equity, an open-end mortgage generally permits a homeowner to borrow up to 80 percent of the current value of the property, which is usually much higher than the value when the original mortgage was drafted.

Suppose a homeowner has paid off about $7,000 of an original $25,000 mortgage, He asks that the open-end provision be honored for that $7,000, plus another $5,000 based on the appreciation of the property since the original $25,000 mortgage was taken out. The lender recognizes the increased value of the house and agrees to add the $12,000 to the existing mortgage, bringing the total loan up to $30,000.

The borrower, however, must accept the lender's current interest rate on the full $30,000, and he or she probably will not receive all the equity and appreciated value that is available via a completely new mortgage. On the other hand, he or she pays the point service fee (the one or two percent charged by the lender to make the loan) only on the $12,000 additional borrowing. And since the title company has only a partial title search to do, the person obtaining an open-end mortgage pays a fee that is lower than would be the case for a full title search.

Wraparound Mortgages

A VARIATION of the open-end mortgage that is especially appealing when the interest rate is low is what is known as a "wraparound mortgage." The extra money that the homeowner wants or needs is provided by a loan that "wraps around" the original mortgage without disturbing it. A second lender assumes payments on the original mortgage and gives the homeowner a new loan, covering the original mortgage and the additional money desired, at an interest rate that is lower than the current market rate.

Consider, for example, a homeowner with a six percent mortgage that still has 15 years to run on a 30-year term. The homeowner likes the low interest rate, but he or she wants to obtain some of the equity and appreciation accumulated over the first 15 years of the mortgage. The idea is to find a lender (private or institutional) who, in addition to assuming the obligation of making payments on the original mortgage until it is paid off, will agree to provide a loan of up to 80 percent of the current value of the home. Finding such a lender can be difficult. The borrower should expect to get a lower overall interest rate (generally about one percent) than is currently being charged for home mortgages because the new lender is paying off the old loan at only six percent.

A wraparound mortgage is often worth the effort to obtain, as long as the original mortgage documents indicate that the initial obligation can be assumed by a second party. Most mortgages dating from the 1950's and early 1960's permitted such assumption, but after 1966 lenders began to insist upon writing new

mortgages at higher rates every time a property was sold.

The Second Mortgage

ONE APPROACH to refinancing that is very common today is the second mortgage. Because it entails greater risk on the part of the lender, however, the second mortgage is substantially more expensive than other forms of refinancing.

Here is how a second mortgage works. A lender agrees to make an additional loan on the appraised value of a home (up to 80 percent) minus the remaining debt owed to the first mortgage lender. For example, if a homeowner still owes $15,000 of a first mortgage on a home appraised currently at $55,000, a second mortgage lender might provide 80 percent of the $40,000 difference between the current appraised value and the balance owed on the first mortgage. The second mortgage, therefore, would amount to $32,000.

The second mortgage allows a homeowner to keep the first mortgage undisturbed. The original mortgage lender is not really affected by a homeowner's second mortgage arrangement and usually need not even be consulted about it. If the property has to be foreclosed by the second creditor because the borrower has failed to meet his obligations, the first mortgage holder will get paid off first.

The disadvantage for the borrower is that the second mortgage is made at an interest rate that is typically three percent higher than the rate that could be obtained on a new first mortgage. The increase in rate is to compensate the second mortgage holder for the additional risk assumed if the property goes into default or if it declines in value. Should either happen, the second lender then has to pay off the first lender before getting anything back on a sale of the collateral residence.

Second-mortgage money is available from all types of lenders except savings and loan associations. Credit unions often offer particularly good terms, but banks and finance companies are prepared to lend second-mortgage money on the increased value of a house.

A second mortgage can be quite useful in certain circumstances. Consider the case of an owner of property appraised at $40,000 with a mortgage obtained during the period of the early 1970's when seven percent home loans were available. To refinance all of the $25,000 still owed on the property, the homeowner would have to accept a current interest rate of nine percent. Since the borrower needs only $6,000, however, he or she goes to a second mortgage lender and asks for the $6,000 plus $1,000 to cover expenses, offering the value of the home as collateral.

The lender finds that the property is indeed worth $40,000 and calculates that 80 percent of the appraised value — or $32,000 — minus the remaining debt owed on the first mortgage — $25,000 — equals the amount that the homeowner wants to borrow. Therefore, the lender agrees to provide the $7,000 with a 12 percent second mortgage. Although the rate is steep, the borrower actually comes out in better shape with a second mortgage than if he or she were to refinance the original mortgage in order to get the extra $7,000. To refinance the entire amount would mean paying nine percent on a much larger loan, plus about two percent in service charges and fees. It is clearly better to pay 12 percent on only a small portion of the debt than nine percent on all of it.

With a second mortgage, however, the borrower incurs a second monthly payment instead of the single monthly payment for refinancing the whole debt. The double payments might well amount to more than the homeowner can afford. But there may even be a way around that stumbling block. The borrower can frequently arrange to pay only the interest each month. Eventually, after a specified number of years, the borrower pays off the principal in one lump sum, usually referred to as a "balloon." Balloon arrangements are quite common today, with many lenders willing to set up such a deferred payment structure.

The borrower profits from a balloon payment arrangement through reduced monthly outlays along with simultaneous use of the money obtained from the second mortgage loan. If he or she invests wisely, there should be no trouble in paying off the balloon note when it comes due several years later.

Even if the borrower loses that money and the balloon payment comes due, he or she can often refinance the home and pay off both the second mortgage and the old first mortgage. This solution sacrifices the remaining years of the original low-interest mortgage, but it takes care of the debt to the second mortgage holder who otherwise could not be paid the amount due.

A second mortgage usually has a much shorter pay-back term than a first mortgage. Often, it must be repaid in five years, especially if a balloon payment is involved. Some second mortgages, though, can be arranged for more extended terms (10 to 15 years, for example), especially if the lender is a commercial bank.

Prepaying A Mortgage

ANOTHER APPROACH to refinancing, one that some lenders actively encourage, is prepaying the mortgage. Prepayment can actually save a homeowner a considerable amount of interest over the life of a mortgage. For example, an extra $20 a month paid on a mortgage would save a homeowner approximately $10,000 in interest charges over the 25-year

> The burden
> of a second mortgage
> can be reduced
> with a "balloon"
> repayment
> schedule.

loan term. Annual lump-sum payments on the outstanding principal would have approximately the same effect.

Here's a concrete example. A person has a loan of $30,000 at 8.5 percent interest for 25 years. The overall monthly principal and interest payments amount to $241.58. Over 25 years, the actual cost of the $30,000 loan will total $72,474. If, however, the person adds $20 a month to the payments, he or she could repay the $30,000 loan in about 19½ years, with a total outlay of $62,486. Thus, the homeowner who pays an extra $20 a month saves approximately $10,000 over the life of the mortgage.

Prepayment, however, is not a good idea for a homeowner who expects to sell in just a few years after purchasing the property. The advantages to prepayment are based on continual reduction of the outstanding principal; since interest is applied only to the principal outstanding at any given time, a homeowner can save a great deal of the interest charges over the long run by steadily reducing the principal. When the principal will be paid back in just a few years — as happens when an owner sells relatively soon

> Prepayment is generally a profitable procedure only for those owners who live in the same home for a long time.

after buying — the interest saved is minimal, and the owner would probably be better off to put the extra money into a savings account.

"The question becomes academic for many people because the average length of time they live in a house is about five years," says Paul Sims, mortgage officer for Home Federal Savings and Loan of Chicago. "But if you think you are going to live in a home for the full mortgage term, and you have $20 or so extra to spend, it might be best to prepay."

Of course, the tax deduction on annual interest charges will be reduced by prepayment, and the $10,000 savings cited in the example above could not be claimed as tax shelter. Depending on the borrower's tax bracket, that loss of shelter could be substantial.

Prepayment does, however, result in substantial accumulation of equity relatively rapidly. Therefore, it serves as a means of protection against financial emergency; most lenders will rebate the accumulated equity back to the mortgage upon request. Having such a fall-back sum serves the same purpose as disability insurance without the cost of such insurance, and it provides additional security for those individuals who might lose their jobs for one reason or another.

Summing Up

REFINANCING in one form or another represents an excellent way for a homeowner to realize a return on real estate without selling it. Some homeowners, especially those who live in areas where property values have steadily increased for many years, routinely refinance every time the equity in their homes rises sufficiently so that the ratio of the loan to the equity drops below 60 percent. They hike the loan back to 75 percent of the value on a new mortgage, and then they use the money derived thereby for other financial ventures. Of course, such ventures must be profitable to make refinancing worthwhile. It makes little sense to take out loans at 9.0 percent interest unless the money obtained can be made to earn at least 10 percent.

Making Money On Your Home

It is conceivable, of course, that a homeowner would refinance to obtain a lower interest rate. In the credit crunch of 1974-75, for example, interest rates on homes went as high as 10 percent in some areas of the nation. By late 1976, lenders had lowered their rates to 8.25 percent in those same areas. A large drop like that makes refinancing appear extremely attractive. The costs of making the new loan would probably offset the first three years of savings from the lower rate, but after that period the savings would be substantial for many years to come.

From the various ways to refinance property that have been described in this chapter, the homeowner should be able to find one that best fits his or her needs. Each one has its own advantages and disadvantages.

The most basic way to refinance is merely to take out a new mortgage, perhaps bargaining for a lower rate by reducing the ratio of the loan amount to the value of the property — i.e., not mortgaging to the maximum 80 percent. In many cases, the home has increased so much in value since the time the original loan was taken out that the buyer need borrow only 60 percent of its value to have all the cash needed. In addition to obtaining a lower interest rate, the homeowner who borrows against less than 80 percent of the home's value faces much lower monthly payments.

The cheapest way to refinance is probably with the open-end mortgage, which involves adding back the accumulated equity and some portion of the appreciation. The most exotic way may be the wraparound mortgage, in which the lower rate on the assumed loan may well enable the borrower to get a better rate on the total package from a wraparound lender.

The easiest way to refinance a home, however, is to obtain a second mortgage on it. The first mortgage stays exactly as it was — a real advantage if it carries a low interest rate — and the borrower normally has no trouble finding lenders willing to offer a second mortgage for up to 80 percent of the home's current appraised value minus, of course, the outstanding first mortgage debt.

The person who is sure that he or she will stay in the same home for the life of the mortgage (or close to it) may find it best to prepay on the equity a little at a time, then reclaim that amount if and when it is needed. Prepayment works well for people who have a little extra income and who can comfortably reduce the mortgage principal on a systematic basis. These people are reducing their interest outlay on the mortgage by a surprising amount while keeping equity funds in reserve.

Refinancing has its disadvantages, too. Taking out a new mortgage entails expenses like a probable increase in interest rates plus service fees. The new loan will usually require larger monthly payments, a result of the increased interest rate and the larger loan taken out on the home's appreciated value.

The open-end mortgage probably will not return all the equity and appreciated value one could receive via a completely new mortgage. The open-end arrangement also requires that the whole mortgage amount be renegotiated at the current interest rate, which usually means a higher interest charge.

In the case of a wraparound mortgage, the basic disadvantage is that the original loan may not be assumable. And finding a lender who understands the wraparound device and is willing to make a loan on that basis can often be a difficult task.

A second mortgage is costly because the interest rate is substantially higher, and it also usually covers only a short term. The higher cost means that the borrower must face a large increase in monthly real estate payments.

Prepaying a mortgage also has its drawbacks. It requires the use of money that might be used more profitably for other purposes. In fact, if the property owner does not intend to keep the property for most or all of the loan term, then he or she is usually better off just depositing those extra funds in a savings account.

A homeowner interested in refinancing should begin by studying his or her mortgage document, checking to see whether it has open-end features, whether it is assumable, and whether it includes a prepayment penalty clause. Then, the owner should talk to a lender. Some refinancing plans can be very advantageous to the lender as well, especially any that will relieve the institution of a loan carrying an interest rate that is low by current standards.

Before signing any refinancing papers, however, the homeowner should talk to several lenders about what he or she is trying to accomplish. This procedure will provide a check against any one lender, and a comparative survey of the market is always to the advantage of the person buying any goods or services.

Most important of all, the homeowner who is considering refinancing must have a plan for using the money obtained for some profitable purpose. An accountant can be very helpful in this regard, informing the owner of tax advantages and offering counsel as to the best refinancing plan to choose. The accountant may also advise holding onto the current mortgage in its present condition because even though refinancing is an important financial tool, it is not one that should be utilized indiscriminately.

How One Homeowner Found Profits In Refinancing

THE ORIGINAL mortgage lender on Ron Davis' property in Atlanta gave him the idea for refinancing his home by sending out a letter to all borrowers suggesting that they consider taking advantage of their homes' increased value. The lender would agree to refinance up to 80 percent of the current appraised value of these homes.

Davis had been trying to figure out how to finance a new business idea, and the circular from his lender was most welcome. He had purchased his $35,000 home in 1971, and now he figured it was worth at least $50,000. A loan equivalent to 80 percent of the value an appraiser put on his home would amount to $40,000, out of which Davis would pay off the old mortgage. In addition, he planned to pull out the $2,500 he had accumulated in equity over the six years since purchase.

Davis contacted the savings and loan association, and he and his wife were cordially invited to come in and provide the necessary information for refinancing.

That information included current income (both were fully employed) and credit data. A couple of days later, an appraiser from the savings and loan association showed up to inspect the home. He spent about 10 minutes at the property and took a few pictures.

Shortly thereafter, Davis received a letter stating that his home had been appraised at $49,000 and that the savings and loan association was prepared to finance 80 percent of that amount or $39,200. The lender required a new survey and raised the 8.5 percent interest rate on the old mortgage up to 8.75 percent on the new loan.

"We got all the information together, then went to closing," Davis said. "There was a week's waiting period, and then I went by and got the check."

Davis had managed to acquire almost 12,000 untaxed dollars from his home, an amount that he immediately invested in a business that promised a much greater return than the 8.75 percent he would have to pay in interest on the higher loan.

Rent For Profit

RENTING OUT A home instead of selling it can be a very attractive alternative to a home investor. It is certainly one of the least utilized options, although it offers several distinct advantages.

- The tax advantages available through renting out a home are even greater than in regular ownership and occupancy because a home used as an investment is assumed by the government to depreciate as it gets older. Of course, homes that are rented rarely wear out in the time frame the government allows. Some stand for 200 years, gaining value every day while simultaneously providing a tax deduction for depreciation.

- The owner of a rented home does not give up any of the tax advantages of ownership. Interest on the mortgage and real estate taxes continue to be deductible. And since there is no sale involved, there is no capital gains tax liability if the owner does not buy another principal residence of equal or higher value within 18 months. This factor can be extremely important to people who want to move to a much less valuable property than the home they own.

- The owner of a rented home continues to enjoy the appreciation in value that the real estate market has been providing. Therefore, when a sale is finally consummated, if ever, the profit will be even greater than when the property was first rented out.

- The owner can continue to make improvements that will add value to the home and bring higher rents. Every time the property is vacant between renters, some capital improvement can be undertaken to increase the home's value. Many times, moreover, tenants will make significant improvements (especially in landscaping) at their own expense.

- Becoming a landlord involves little ex-
pense. There is no financing involved, and standard lease forms are available at stationery stores. The fee for an accountant to figure taxable income (or loss) is deductible, as are the charges for the minimal advice, if any, needed from an attorney.

- The costs of finding a suitable renter are generally minor. In most areas of the country, the scarcest commodity in the real estate market is rental property, especially single-family homes. With many people staying in one place for only a year or two, the demand for rental space has accelerated. Many of these renters will pay extra to rent a home rather than an apartment, especially if the home is in a good school district.

- Most importantly, the owner's monthly mortgage payments can be offset by the rental income. In fact, a home with an older mortgage at a low interest rate can often bring in rental income that is substantially more than the mortgage payments, thereby putting cash in the owner's pocket.

Naturally, such a splendid investment vehicle has some weaknesses.

- The owner is expected to handle the tenant's problems with the home and to pay for any repairs when there is a breakdown. This responsibility can constitute a considerable drain on the owner's time and financial resources, especially if he or she is not handy enough to take care of minor repairs.

- The tenant could damage the property to such an extent that it actually loses value. Even by failing to keep up the lawn or letting trees and shrubs die or neglecting routine maintenance chores a tenant can force the owner to spend a great deal of money in order to put the property back in shape.

- Many property owners don't like renters living in their neighborhood because renters frequently fail to maintain property as well as the owners do. Both landlord and renter must live with the fact that neighbors may not approve of the basic living arrangement, fearing that their own property values will suffer.

- Sometimes rents don't cover all the expenses of ownership; this is especially true in condominiums where the association assessments usually are paid by the unit owner. If the assessment sum is substantial, it — when added to the mortgage payments — may result in a negative situation for the owner. And there is a limit, of course, to which rents can be raised to cover expenses.

- Finally, the homeowner may not be able to buy another residence to live in without obtaining the equity from the present home. Simultaneous ownership of two homes may seem financially impossible.

Fortunately, all of the negative aspects of renting can be overcome or at least moderated.

One More Advantage

THE OWNER of rental property enjoys one further potential advantage: The government considers a rented home to be investment real estate which can be exchanged for other investment real estate. And since the government does not consider an exchange to be taxable (unless cash is involved or unless a more valuable property is acquired for immediate sale), no capital gains tax applies to the real estate involved.

Real estate brokers know of many creative ways to transact tax-free exchanges. Home rental is just the first step, but it is an important step in establishing the property as investment real estate. Starting with their own homes, many investors have built real estate portfolios of several income-producing properties.

Renting a home provides an owner with many of the experiences of handling larger properties. It's a good place to begin to get an education in figuring depreciation, evaluating tenants, dealing with leases, determining rents, setting up income and expense statements, understanding tenant-landlord relationships, and learning other lessons that will prove beneficial when it comes time to get into more complicated real estate transactions.

A True Growth Investment

HOME INVESTOR Sidney Miller's financial situation looks better every year. When he first converted his home to rental property, he said, "I don't even expect any cash from this investment. I just want the rental income to cover the mortgage payments and the maintenance costs. I'm counting on the annual appreciation of 5 to 10 percent that has been occurring in the home market plus the tax advantages to make money for me."

Miller has realized much more than that — so much more, in fact, that he has purchased several more houses for rental. Since his first purchase in the early 1970's, his property appreciation has averaged 12 percent a year. He has

> Renting out a home has the potential for being a splendid investment vehicle.

raised the rent on the initial home from $300 to $450 a month, and he has no trouble getting tenants to pay it.

Here is a breakdown of how Miller's property has become a good growth investment.

For 1973

Mortgage payments (12×$275)	$3,300
Maintenance expenses	$650
Total costs of renting out the home	$3,950
Income from tenant (12×$300)	$3,600
Net loss before taxes	$350

For 1977

Mortgage payments (12×$275)	$3,300
Maintenance expenses	$850
Total costs of renting out the home	$4,150
Income from tenant (12×$450)	$5,400
Net gain before taxes	$1,250

Thus Miller has moved from a net loss before taxes (which, however, was deductible on his income taxes) to about a 30 percent return. The depreciation he can claim as an investment property owner (but not as an owner-occupant of the same home) enables him to shelter most of that income so that it becomes pure untaxed profit. He also continues to receive the tax benefits of deductible interest and real estate taxes, and his home has risen in value by about 40 percent during this period.

The stability of mortgage payments is one of the key factors here. When a person finances real estate, the mortgage costs are set for the whole term of the loan, unless the mortgage is refinanced. That stability to someone who both owns and lives in a home is not a crucial factor. To someone who rents out the property, however, that stability means almost a dollar of profit for every dollar the rent can be raised. In other words, it's a simple matter of boosting income without raising expenses.

Maintenance costs can be counted on to increase, of course; inflation takes care of that.

As a home ages, moreover, it tends to require more expensive repairs and replacements. No one who is thinking of renting out a home can afford to overlook that replacement of a roof or repair of a furnace can wipe out any profit in a given year. On the other hand, such costs are tax deductible for investment property.

The Vacancy Question

ANOTHER CRITICAL factor is vacancy. Obviously, a landlord who has no renter for several months receives no income to cover expenses. It is vital, therefore, that the owner who rents out a home know the intentions of a tenant as long before the end of the lease as possible.

In fact, it could be said that knowing one's tenants is the key to prosperity as a landlord. The smart owner doesn't rent to just anybody; he or she is willing to go to great lengths to check out the people who will occupy his or her home. There are people who are careless and even destructive, and owners must be very careful to select tenants who take pride in a home even though it is a rental property. Real estate authorities claim that the best way to upgrade a property is to upgrade the caliber of people who live there, and a good tenant will not only maintain but increase the value of a home in which he or she lives.

There are several ways to check on a prospective tenant. One is the credit check that property managers of larger buildings regard as a standard procedure. The cost of such a check usually runs between $50 and $100. Another involves asking the would-be tenant for the name of the landlord before the current one. Rather than cause the tenant a problem in the building he or she is about to leave, the owner should go one landlord back for information. Landlords (or their property managers) usually are quite candid about what kind of tenant the prospect had been, and because the tenant is no longer in their building, they can be objective.

Nothing, however, is better than the one-to-one interview in evaluating a prospective tenant. Knowing what kind of job he or she has,

**After finding
a good tenant,
setting the rent
is the next
crucial step
for the
homeowner/landlord.**

Managing The Rental Property

THE LANDLORD certainly is responsible for plumbing or mechanical failures, a flooded basement, leaky roof, and other major break-downs, and he or she must know whom to call in an emergency to get the problem fixed promptly. A tenant, even more than a homeowner, is impatient about breakdowns. Therefore, the owner must know good, efficient service people who can take care of needed repairs without delay — and of course at a fair price. A landlord who keeps a list of qualified tradesmen and service people with business and emergency numbers can respond immediately when the tenant calls.

There are other aspects to managing a rental property of which the owner must be aware. He or she should collect a security deposit as a safeguard against damages that the tenant might do to the property during residence; this deposit is usually returned after deducting the costs of repairing any damages. The tenant should be given a rental statement on the first day of the month, and he or she must be given notice of cancellation of the lease; 30 to 60 days is the legal requirement in most states.

Setting The Rent

THE MOST IMPORTANT management job for the owner is, of course, setting the rent so that the home will attract tenants on the one hand and contribute as much as possible to offset expenses on the other. Establishing a fair market rent is a tricky business, and it must be repeated every time a lease nears expiration.

Some owners of rental condominiums assume that they can just offer the unit at a price somewhat above their mortgage payments and monthly assessments. They generally face a rude awakening, however, when they find that the price they set is substantially higher than prospective tenants must pay for equivalent ac-commodations in a regular apartment building.

The reason this situation occurs is that rents have not increased as rapidly as have the prices of for-sale property. In fact, rents in the

previous residences, general attitudes about tenant responsibilities, etc., probably tell the most about whether this person or family is right for the home to be rented. In a good rental market, owners have enough potential occu-pants so that they need not accept tenants of doubtful character.

Once the tenant has been selected, it is time to present the lease. The standard lease forms available at stationery stores contain almost all the necessary legal protections for both owner and tenant, but it is drawn up for apartment building rentals and not for a home. It would be advisable, therefore, to obtain an attorney's ad-vice regarding how to specify what areas of maintenance and overall responsibility lie in the owner's domain and which ones a tenant is bound to handle. A lease that spells out each party's obligations can resolve a disagreement quickly and prevent a great many tenant/landlord conflicts.

Sample Residence Lease

DATE OF LEASE	TERM OF LEASE		RENT	SECURITY DEPOSIT*
	BEGINNING	ENDING		

IF NONE, WRITE "NONE"; Paragraph 2 of this Lease then INAPPLICABLE.

LESSEE		**LESSOR**	
NAME	•	NAME	•
ADDRESS OF	•	ADDRESS	•
PREMISES	•	CITY	•
CITY	•		

In consideration of the mutual covenants and agreements herein stated, Lessor hereby leases to Lessee and Lessee hereby leases from Lessor for a private dwelling the house designated above (the "Premises"), together with the appurtenances thereto, for the above term.

RENT

1. Lessee shall pay Lessor as rent for the Premises the sum stated above, monthly in advance, until termination of this lease, at Lessor's address stated above or such other address as Lessor may designate in writing. Time of each such payment is of the essence of this agreement.

SECURITY DEPOSIT

2. Lessee has deposited with Lessor the Security Deposit stated above as security for the performance of all covenants and agreements of Lessee hereunder. Lessor may at any time or times apply all or any portion thereof in payment of any amounts due Lessor from Lessee. Upon termination of the lease and full performance of all of Lessee's obligations hereunder, so much of the Security Deposit as remains unapplied shall be returned to Lessee. The Security Deposit shall not bear interest.

CONDITION OF PREMISES

3. Lessee acknowledges that the Premises are in good repair, except as herein otherwise specified, and that no representations as to the condition or repair thereof have been made by the Lessor, or Lessor's agent, prior to or at the execution of this lease, that are not herein expressed.

REPAIR

4. The Lessee covenants and agrees with Lessor to take good care of and keep in clean and healthy condition the Premises and their fixtures, and to commit or suffer no waste therein; that no changes or alterations of the Premises shall be made or partitions erected, nor walls papered without the consent in writing of Lessor; that Lessee will make all repairs required to the walls, windows, glass, ceilings, paint, plastering, plumbing work, pipes, and fixtures belonging to the Premises, whenever damage or injury to the same shall have resulted from misuse or neglect; and Lessee agrees to pay for any and all repairs that shall be necessary to put the Premises in the same condition as when he entered therein, reasonable wear and loss by fire excepted, and the expense of such repairs shall be included within the terms of this lease and any judgment by confession entered therefor.

LIMITATION OF LIABILITY

5. The Lessor shall not be liable for any damage occasioned by failure to keep the Premises in repair, and shall not be liable for any damage done or occasioned by or from plumbing, gas, water, steam, or other pipes, sewerage, or the bursting, leaking or running from any cistern, tank, washstand, water closet or waste pipe in, above, upon or about the Premises, nor for damage occasioned by water, snow or ice, being upon or coming through the roof, skylight, trap door or otherwise, nor for any damage arising from acts or neglect of any owners or occupants of adjacent or contiguous property.

USE; SUBLET; ASSIGNMENT

6. Lessee will not allow the Premises to be used for any purpose that will increase the rate of insurance thereon, nor for any purpose other than that hereinbefore specified, nor to be occupied, in whole or in part, by any other person, and will not sublet the same, or any part thereof, nor assign this lease, without in each case the Lessor's written consent had, and will not permit and transfer, by operation of law, of the interest in the Premises acquired through this lease; and will not permit the Premises to be used for unlawful purpose or purposes that will injure the reputation of the same or of the neighborhood; will keep no dogs, cats or other animals or pets in or about the Premises; will not permit the Premises to remain vacant or unoccupied for more than ten consecutive days; and will not permit any alteration of or upon any part of the Premises, nor allow any signs or placards posted or placed thereon, except by written consent of the Lessor; all alterations and additions to the Premises shall remain for the benefit of the Lessor unless otherwise provided in said consent.

RIGHT TO RELET

7. If Lessee shall abandon or vacate the Premises, the same shall be re-let by the Lessor for such rent, and upon such terms as Lessor may see fit; and if a sufficient sum shall not be thus realized, after paying the expenses of such re-letting and collecting, to satisfy the rent hereby reserved, the Lessee agrees to satisfy and pay all deficiency.

HOLDING OVER

8. If the Lessee retains possession of the Premises or any part thereof after the termination of the term by lapse of time or otherwise, then the Lessor may at Lessor's option within thirty days after the termination of the term serve written notice upon Lessee that such holding over constitutes either (a) renewal of this lease for one year, and from year to year thereafter, at double the rental specified under Section 1 for such period, or (b) creation of a month to month tenancy, upon the terms of this lease except at double the monthly rental specified under Section 1, or (c) creation of a tenancy at sufferance, at a rental of

_____dollars per day for the time Lessee remains in possession. If no such written notice is served then a tenancy at sufferance with rental as stated at (c) shall have been created. Lessee shall also pay to Lessor all damages sustained by Lessor resulting from retention of possession by Lessee.

FLAMMABLES

9. Naphtha, benzine, benzole, gasoline, benzine-varnish, gunpowder, fireworks, nitroglycerine, phosphorus, saltpeter, nitrate of soda, camphene, spirit-gas, or any flammable fluid or oil, shall not be allowed or used on the Premises without the written permission of the Lessor.

TAXES AND UTILITIES

10. Lessee shall pay (in addition to the rent above specified) all water taxes and all gas, electricity and power bills, levied or charged on or in respect of the Premises, for and during the term of this lease, and in case no water taxes are levied specifically on or in respect of the Premises, to pay the_____ part of all water taxes levied or charged on or in respect of the building of which the Premises constitutes a part; and in case said water taxes and gas, electricity and power bills shall not be paid when due, Lessor shall have the right to pay the same, which amount so paid, together with any sums paid by Lessor to keep the Premises and their appurtenances in good condition as hereinbefore specified, shall be due and payable with the next installment of rent due thereafter under this lease.

SIGNS

11. Lessor reserves the right to put up a "To Rent" sign sixty days prior to the expiration of this lease and a "For Sale" sign at any time during the term of this lease.

COMPLIANCE

12. Lessee will in every respect comply with the ordinances of the municipality aforesaid, with the rules and orders of the health officers thereof, with the orders and requirements of the police department, with the requirements of any underwriters' association so as not to increase the rates of insurance upon the building and contents thereof, and with the rules and orders of the fire department in respect to any matters coming within their jurisdiction.

DEFAULT

13. If default be made in the payment of the above rent, or any part thereof, or in any of the covenants herein contained to be kept by Lessee, it shall be lawful for Lessor at any time, at his election, without notice, to declare said term ended and to re-enter the Premises, or any part thereof, with or without process of law, and to remove Lessee or any persons occupying the same, without prejudice to any remedies which might otherwise be used for arrears of rent, and Lessor shall have at all times the right to distrain for rent due and shall have a valid and first lien upon all personal property which Lessee owns or may hereafter acquire or have an interest in, whether exempt by law or not, as security for payment of the rent herein reserved.

CONFESSION

14. The Lessee hereby irrevocably constitutes any attorney of any court of record in this state, attorney for Lessee in Lessee's name, on default by Lessee of any of the covenants herein, and upon complaint made by Lessor, his agent or assigns, and filed in any such court to enter Lessee's appearance in any such court of record, waive process and service thereof, and confess judgment, from time to time, for any rent which may be due to Lessor, or the Lessor's assignees, by the terms of this lease, with costs and a reasonable sum for attorney's fees, and to waive all errors and all right of appeal from said judgment, and to consent in writing that a writ of execution may be issued immediately.

RENT AFTER NOTICE OR SUIT

15. After the service of notice, or the commencement of a suit, or after final judgment for possession of the Premises, the Lessor may receive and collect any rent due, and the payment of said rent shall not waive or affect said notice, said suit, or said judgment.

FIRE AND CASUALTY

16. In case the Premises shall be rendered untenantable by fire or other casualty, Lessor may at his option terminate this lease, or repair the Premises within thirty days, and failing so to do, or upon the destruction of the Premises by fire, the term hereby created shall cease and determine.

PAYMENT OF COSTS

17. The Lessee further covenants and agrees to pay and discharge all reasonable costs, attorney's fees and expenses that shall be made and incurred by Lessor in enforcing the covenants and agreements of this lease.

PLURALS; SUCCESSORS

18. The words "Lessor" and "Lessee" wherever herein occurring and used shall be construed to mean "Lessors" and "Lessees" in case more than one person constitutes either party to this lease, and all such persons shall be jointly and severally liable hereon; and all the covenants and agreements herein contained shall be binding upon, and inure to, their respective successors, heirs, executors, administrators and assigns and be exercised by his or their attorney or agent.

SEVER-ABILITY

19. If any clause, phrase, provision or portion of this lease or the application thereof to any person or circumstance shall be invalid, or unenforceable under applicable law, such event shall not affect, impair or render invalid or unenforceable the remainder of this lease nor any other clause, phrase, provision or portion hereof, nor shall it affect the application of any clause, phrase, provision or portion hereof to other persons or circumstances.

WITNESS the hands and seals of the parties hereto, as of the Date of Lease stated above.

_____(SEAL)

_____(SEAL)

GUARANTEE

For value received_____hereby guarantee the payment of the rent and the performance of the covenants by the Lessee in the within lease covenanted and agreed, in manner and form as in said lease provided.

WITNESS_____hand__and seal__this_____day of_____, 19_____.

_____(SEAL)

_____(SEAL)

ASSIGNMENT BY LESSOR

In consideration of One Dollar, to the Lessor in hand paid, the Lessor hereby transfers, assigns and sets over to_____

_____and_____

Successors and assigns Lessor's interest in the within lease, and the rent thereby secured_____

_____

WITNESS_____hand and seal this_____day of_____, 19_____.

_____(SEAL)

_____(SEAL)

NOTE: Use Form Number 12-1 for assignment by Tenant.

United States tend to be a bargain compared to rents in other countries. Fear of rent control, strict management policies, and lower construction costs contribute to keeping rents down. Condominium monthly charges, on the other hand, are generally quite steep due to the addition of amenities, better construction, luxury extras, and more liberal management.

A single-family home is affected by the prevailing rental rates as much as a condominium is. A home, however, usually brings more rent per square foot than a condominium — given equal access to transportation, services, and schools. The yard that a condominium or apartment building lacks is often a big plus, as is the privacy that only a home provides.

The major obstacle to establishing the rent for a home is the relatively limited volume of data. Brokers can render some advice (especially to the owner who uses the broker to find tenants), but appraisers usually don't have this kind of information.

While there is no easy or precise way to establish the rent for a home, there is a reasonably accurate way. The owner should first determine the square footage of the home and then call a few rental apartment buildings in the area that prospective tenants might consider as an alternative to the home for rent. The property managers at these buildings will indicate what the rents are and how much square footage the large apartments (the ones comparable to the home) contain. By checking three such buildings, the owner will begin to get an impression of what price the current rental market will pay for the property in question.

Usually, a home will bring at least 10 percent more in rent than a comparably sized apartment unless the building in which the apartment is located offers exceptional amenities such as an indoor pool, 24-hour security, doorman, commercial facilities, etc. The owner can compare his or her property with what the apartment buildings provide and — given equivalent amenities — tack on 10 percent to the rent for an apartment of comparable size.

The owner will soon know if the price is too high because few prospects will show an interest in a rental home that costs much more than similar rental properties. Fortunately, there is no great problem in being too high in a rental situation as there is in a sale where the brokers and many of the neighbors discover that the owner cannot get his or her price. A rental is more private, and the owner can reduce the original rental price without suffering any loss except time.

By the same token, pricing too low is also not as injurious as it is in a sale. When the lease expires, the owner merely hikes the rent to the level it should be. Perhaps the tenant enjoyed a year or two at bargain rates (and he or she probably knows it), but the owner possesses the ability to adjust the rent upward in order to get what the home is really worth.

During both the initial pricing of a rented home and in raising the rent at a later date, the owner should examine closely the classified ads for rental housing, especially those for homes in the area. In fact, by clipping out rental ads for nearby homes and apartment buildings the owner can maintain a continuous record of how much additional rent apartment managers are writing into new leases. The rent on comparable homes and the length of time the ads run provide valuable information in determining the highest rent acceptable to the market.

The best homes to rent out, according to Chicago home investment advisor Morris Replogle, are those that would sell for $30,000 to $50,000. "When you get up to rents for $60,000 to $70,000 homes, you find that many people who could afford those rents would prefer to buy. In the lower price ranges, you have a great number of potential tenants who want the space and privacy of a house instead of an apartment. They'll pay more than an apartment renter to get those things."

Financing A Second Home

THE DRAWBACK for many people who would like to rent their homes is that they simply cannot afford to buy another residence without acquiring the equity from their current home. In many cases, however, these people are unaware of the many financing techniques that exist to overcome their problems. Here are a few of those techniques.

- Use the accumulated equity and appreciation in the first home as the basis for asking a lender to consider a 90 percent or even a 95 percent loan on the new property. The lender will see that the homeowner has a substantial asset, one that offers the potential of returning an income, and may be willing to do some creative financing to help the owner realize his or her objectives.

- Obtain a second mortgage on the property to be rented in whatever amount is needed for a downpayment on the property to be purchased. For example, an owner of a home valued at $45,000 with $20,000 left on the mortgage could obtain a second mortgage of $12,000 to be used as a 20 percent downpayment on a home worth up to $60,000. If the second mortgage includes a balloon payment of the principal, moreover, the owner might only pay interest for 8 to 10 years and realize enough in tax benefits and cash return on the rental property to cover the entire $12,000 loan when it comes due.

- Refinance to get the needed capital out of the first home. But if refinancing involves the loss of a low-interest mortgage, it might reduce the return from renting to such an extent as to make the venture unprofitable.

- Use private mortgage insurance to cover the top 10 percent of a 90 percent mortgage; the owner then must come up with just 10 percent down on the new property. That amount can often be obtained by borrowing against other assets or insurance without involving the property to be rented.

One Note Of Caution

IN DECIDING whether to rent out property or not, the homeowner must also consider one

> Renting out
> a home
> can be
> quite profitable
> as long as
> property values
> remain
> on the upswing.

other important real estate factor: Does the neighborhood seem to be steadily improving? Some rental experts think subdivision homes make the best rentals because a tract development starts out with little or no landscaping, with amenities that are still to be delivered, and with many owners who still have their high income days in front of them. As the subdivision turns into a neighborhood with trees and flowers, schools and recreational facilities, and the income level of the owners is high enough that they can spend more money on their property, values will be increasing much more rapidly than in older and more established neighborhoods.

Ironically, the areas where rental is not advisable are those where more and more homes are being rented. A neighborhood retains its stability when only a few homes are rented. A trend to rental often causes property values to suffer, and a homeowner who detects such a trend should sell the property rather than continue to rent it out.

In summary, renting for profit makes a good deal of sense for many investors. It can return both real income and tax shelter, a combination that few other investments available to the small investor can duplicate.

Profit By Selling

Making Money On Your Home

IN MANY SITUATIONS, the most sensible thing an owner can do with a home is to sell it. For example, the timing may be just right for a sale — i.e., when tight money conditions are anticipated but not yet a reality.

What a seller needs in order to realize maximum profit is a large supply of qualified buyers who have access to mortgage money at attractive terms. A seller can then feel reasonably confident that someone in that supply of qualified buyers will pay top dollar for the property and will be able to find a lender with plenty of money to finance it.

That supply of potential buyers is greatly reduced, however, when tight money conditions occur. During a period in 1974-75, for example, many leading institutions were taking in so little money from savers that they refused to make home loans to anyone other than their best customers, and then they did so only at rates of 9 percent or higher. In many cases, these lending institutions insisted that borrowers make a downpayment of 30 percent (or more) of the value of the property before consenting to mortgage the remaining 70 percent at a high rate of interest.

As if sellers of existing homes didn't have enough problems during that credit crunch period, they were further beset by the builders of new homes who had just come off a record production year. Having built more homes than they could sell, these builders cut prices, gave away automobiles and free trips, and succeeded in attracting many prospects who would normally have purchased existing rather than new housing.

Builders of new homes did something else that exacerbated the already troubled market for existing homes. They drained off much of the available mortgage money by calling in financing arranged before the crunch and by using their clout with lenders to arrange mortgages for their new buyers. These lenders were obligated to the builders because the builders had been good customers before the money situation had deteriorated.

It was a classic example of how the shortage of mortgage money can interrupt the rise in value of real estate. Home prices did not decline like the prices for undeveloped land and industrial real estate did, but the steady appreciation in home values — which had been averaging 6 to 8 percent a year — stopped abruptly.

By selling before the supply of mortgage money becomes so constricted, the smart homeowner follows one bit of sound real estate advice: Sell in the good times and hold through the bad. The truth of this adage has been proven repeatedly through the six money cycle changes that have occurred since 1965.

What happens if a homeowner guesses wrong and sells when no money shortage is imminent? The value of the home continues to escalate, which means that a higher price could probably have been obtained by holding the property longer. On the other hand, the seller who reinvests the proceeds from the sale in a new home — which is usually the case — loses nothing by trying to read the signs of an impending credit crunch. In fact, if the new home is a more expensive property, the homeowner will actually derive greater dollar growth through appreciation of a more valuable residence.

Smart sellers
put homes on the market
right before
credit conditions
get tight.

Another instance in which selling makes good sense occurs when property values in the present community or neighborhood seem to be stabilizing while values are escalating in other areas. The wise home investor keeps a constant check on where values are rising fastest and buys in a rapidly appreciating area when the present community becomes relatively stagnant. Even real estate that has shown a nice, steady gain each year should often be sold in order for the owner to get into a hotter area.

The best time to sell an existing home and buy a newly built one is when homebuilders are offering their lowest prices. By watching what is happening in the industry, an investor can detect trends that will pay off handsomely in the future.

For example, builders enjoyed an excellent sales year in 1977, one of the best years homebuilders had ever experienced. Sales started to soar during the fall of 1976 (usually a slow season for new home sales), and it was easy to predict that 1977 would be a good year, especially since mortgage interest rates were relatively low.

The sales boom in new homes, however, created shortages of materials and labor as well as land ready for development. Consequently, by the end of 1977, builders were paying up to 20 percent more for these items than they were at the start of the year. Since the prices they charged had to cover these costs, increases in home prices of 12 to 18 percent were common within a one year period. People who purchased their new homes in late 1976 or early 1977, therefore, saw their property become significantly more valuable in a single year as builders began charging much higher prices for the identical property.

Clearly, it pays to watch what happens in the new home industry and to buy in probable growth areas when homebuilders offer attractive terms. The ultimate profit from such a purchase can far exceed that which can be derived by holding onto an existing home in a less volatile area.

All of this advice assumes that the seller has

Think about selling whenever the rate of appreciation in home values seems to stagnate in relation to other areas.

plenty of time to choose the most advantageous moment to take the profit in his or her home. If that luxury is available, it pays dividends to sell when at least one of the following conditions is existent:

- Before an impending shortage of credit.
- When the rate of value appreciation for the present home falls below that of homes in other desirable areas.
- When cost increases for new homes seem likely to drive up prices.

What about the people who don't have all the time in the world to choose the most propitious moment to sell? What should a homeowner do who must make a quick decision when a better property becomes available or when a transfer to a new area is imminent and unavoidable? Fortunately, there are ways to maximize the profit from a sale in these circumstances as well.

Making Money On Your Home

Avoiding The Double-Mortgage Squeeze

THE LOWMAN FAMILY faced two problems shortly after Mr. Lowman was transferred from Memphis to Chicago — the mortgage payments on their unsold property back in Tennessee and the mortgage payments on their new home in a Chicago suburb. As it turned out, their home in Memphis took more than eight months to sell, and the Lowmans had to endure the nightmare of paying a total of $1,250 a month on two mortgage loans.

The double-mortgage squeeze can happen and often does when people buy a new house before selling their old home. Sometimes, the timing of the purchase just doesn't permit a prior sale of the previous residence. Another way one can get caught in this squeeze occurs when a buyer changes his or her mind at the last minute after the seller is committed to another purchase. Or, as happened to the Lowmans, the sale period can coincide with a time when mortgage money is extremely hard to obtain. Many prospective buyers of the Lowman home either could not find financing or decided to wait until interest rates declined.

There are several ways to guard against ending up with two mortgages. One is to have a contingency clause in the contract to buy the new home which states, in effect, that the purchase will occur only after the present residence is sold. A good device in a market where the seller knows that buyers are scarce, the contingency clause provides protection against simultaneous ownership of two homes.

In a seller's market, however, where there is plenty of buying activity, few owners will agree to hold a home off the market for the convenience of a prospective purchaser. Builders of new homes often will go along with a contingency clause if they have a big inventory of homes, but it's not in the best interests of an individual seller in a good market to offer this type of protection to a buyer.

Another device is the deferred closing date. It's a more reasonable type of contingency clause that most sellers are willing to accept as part of the contract. In effect, this clause sets a closing date that gives the buyer 60 to 90 days to sell the previous home. In a normal market, that length of time should be enough for the buyer to sell his or her home.

People who are truly trapped in a double-mortgage squeeze should go to their lending institutions for help. Frequently, a lender can arrange an interest-only interim loan on the new house that will be replaced with an interest-plus-principal permanent loan when the transactions on both houses have closed. A lender is most likely to go along with this plan if the borrower's previous home has a contract on it and closing will occur before very long.

If owning two homes simultaneously poses a serious threat to the owner's finances and selling the old house seems unlikely for sometime to come, he or she could rent out the previous residence to cover the mortgage payments. The rental market has been so strong in most of the country that renters are generally easy to find, even on short-term or cancellable (with perhaps 60 days notice) leases. The renter, moreover, might actually decide to purchase the property after living in the home.

Refinancing the old house and using the appreciation as a downpayment on the new represents another way to buy a new home before selling the old one. Here's an example. A house purchased seven years ago for $50,000 currently has a mortgage balance of $40,000. During the seven years the house appreciated so that it is presently worth $75,000. The lender refinances the home with a new 80 percent mortgage, giving the owner $40,000 to pay off the old mortgage plus more than $20,000 to use as downpayment on the new home. The borrower continues to pay the interest on the refinanced mortgage until the home is sold, after which he or she pays off the $60,000 borrowed in the refinancing.

If a lender regards both homes as having good value, he may agree to a lower downpayment on the purchase of the new home. In this way, a borrower can come up with a sufficient downpayment even before getting the equity out of the previous property. For example, instead of demanding a downpayment of

20 percent, the lender might agree to take just 5 or 10 percent on the new purchase and then renegotiate the loan after the borrower acquires equity from the eventual sale of the old home. Although a deal of this nature allows for the purchase of a new home prior to the sale of the old one, it does not rescue a buyer/seller from the nightmare of the double-mortgage squeeze.

A wraparound mortgage sometimes can be negotiated as a form of refinancing that allows the buyer/seller to refinance the old home and to finance the new one under the same loan. The lender will usually require the borrower to pay only the interest, replacing this temporary mortgage with a standard loan as soon as the old home is sold. As in refinancing, however, the buyer/seller faces the expense of closing costs both when the temporary financing is arranged and again when the permanent loan is provided.

"The trouble with these remedies is that practically all of them are likely to cost money and not all of them are available all of the time in all markets," points out John Domeier, President of Great American Federal Savings and Loan Association. Therefore, Domeier advocates doing everything possible to avoid getting caught in the double-mortgage squeeze in the first place.

There are
several ways
to avoid
the double-mortgage
squeeze, but
most of them
cost money.

Pricing The Home For Sale

PRICING IT RIGHT is a key factor in selling the home without undue delay and thereby avoiding a double-mortgage situation. A broker can offer good advice about pricing, but a seller should not feel obliged to accept that advice. The best approach is for the owner to do some checking on his or her own. A broker can furnish current listings for similar homes and provide information regarding recent sales of comparable properties. With information of this type, an owner can determine whether a projected price is on target.

The savings and loan association in the area also has a considerable amount of useful data. Appraisers at these institutions are as familiar with recent sales in the area as brokers are. In fact, appraisers at savings and loans often can — for a fee — provide a seller with an appraisal to show to a prospective buyer; an objective evaluation of this sort can be quite convincing in a sales presentation if a prospect insists that the property is overpriced or merely wants confirmation that the home represents a sound purchase. Since the savings and loan appraiser works almost exclusively in the area that the institution services, he is probably better informed about recent sales than an independent appraiser would be, and his fee generally is lower than an independent charges.

Brokers advocate that the owner price a home so that he or she receives market value — that is, what a typical buyer would pay a typical seller for a property that has been exposed to the market for a reasonable period of time. Certainly, an owner should accept no less than market value, and it is thus a good strategy to list a home for sale at about 10 percent above the price of comparable homes sold recently in the area. By the time the owner's home is sold, the market value might actually be 10 percent higher; home prices can escalate that rapidly in just a few months.

Pricing the home a bit above market value could, of course, result in a sale at that level to some buyer who is especially taken with the property and willing to pay extra for it. Then that difference between the sales price and the market value becomes pure profit in the seller's pocket.

More importantly, though, it is essential to allow some room for negotiation about the final price. The prospective buyer will usually make an offer several thousand dollars under the list price, and negotiations start at the level of the buyer's offer. A home listed at a price equivalent to its market value cannot be negotiated without sacrificing some of its actual worth.

The Owner-Sold Home

SELLING A HOME oneself calls for a different strategy. Most of the sales figures for homes sold recently in the area probably include the 6 to 7 percent commission that went to the brokers who handled the transactions. Thus, an owner who sells his or her home at an equivalent price is receiving much more than market value for the property. Prospective buyers, though, know when they are dealing with an owner directly, and they often negotiate harder in order to share in the little windfall that the owner is attempting to reap.

The important thing about selling a home oneself is that the process should not be allowed to fail. An owner never wants to have to go to a broker with a home that has been on the market several weeks or months without selling. In the process of not selling, the property acquires something of a stigma. In addition, an owner in this position can hardly raise the price in order to recover either the broker's commission or any value appreciation that the area might have enjoyed since the home first went on the market. At this point, the owner is forced to sell the home at the best price possible — which may well have fallen due to the home being on the market for some time — and then must pay the broker's commission.

The idea, therefore, is to move the property as quickly as possible. Since the do-it-yourself seller generally doesn't have as many prospects to deal with as when a broker is supplying the potential buyers, the home must be attractively priced. Ten percent above market value

is probably too high for an owner-sold home; just slightly above market value is more realistic.

Among the many headaches that the do-it-yourself seller faces is screening prospects before allowing them inside to tour the home. Fortunately, a great deal of screening can be accomplished over the telephone. The seller should be prepared to tell callers what the downpayment and monthly payments would be for a loan on 80 percent of the estimated value of the home. Inquiring callers should be asked whether they have the income and downpayment to qualify. The seller should explain that the only purpose in requesting this information is to avoid wasting everyone's time by showing a home that is beyond the buyer's means.

It is always a good idea for the owner to have a second person present in the home — the sales agent serves that purpose if the owner utilizes a real estate broker — when showing the property to a prospect. Sadly, some individuals with criminal intentions pose as buyers in order to gain easy entry into a home. That danger must be considered by the owner trying to sell a home without a broker.

Many of the other functions that a broker provides, however, can be handled quite easily by the owner. The broker does advertise the property, but there is no special mystery to describing a home in an advertisement in the local newspaper's classified section. The advertising department of the publication will help word the ad if the owner needs assistance, but a quick review of the home ads in the paper generally provides about all the guidance anyone really needs.

Since most sales are made to people who live within 10 miles of the property, owners should first place ads in the most popular community papers. The rates are usually cheaper than a metropolitan daily charges, and therefore an owner can take out a larger ad without spending any more money. On the other hand, the metropolitan papers reach many more people, and the owner should switch to that larger readership if the community paper fails to produce satisfactory results.

Brokers claim that they handle all the paperwork and details after the buyer is found, but an attorney employed by the do-it-yourself seller does the same thing. The attorney draws up the sales contract, holds the buyer's deposit in a trust account, and completes the details of closing. The fee for an attorney's services can run from $150 to $300, depending on the complexity of the transaction. Since a lawyer is highly desirable (if not a necessity) whenever a person sells a home, however, the owner would pay that fee whether or not a broker's services were utilized.

Selling Through A Broker

THOSE EXTRA DOLLARS that an owner acquires by not using a broker can be quite substantial, and do-it-yourself selling is therefore quite tempting. Sellers who live in areas where homes are sold soon after going on the market should probably try to go it alone, but there are good reasons for using a broker in certain situations even though that means paying the sizable sales commission.

A seller who is in a hurry to unload a home — even if the market is relatively good — is frequently wise to use a broker. It is very possible that the broker knows of a buyer looking for just the home in question. In fact, the real estate agent's greatest service to the owner requiring a quick sale is familiarity with the needs and desires of a great many buyers. A do-it-yourselfer may be unable to reach these potential buyers or to motivate them to come and look at the property as effectively as a real estate agent can.

Many brokers, moreover, are tied into a network with brokers in other major cities, which means that they have access to prospective buyers — i.e., transferred employees — that might never see an advertisement for a home in a community newspaper. Transferees represent a significant portion of the home sales market, and they usually come into an area with a limited amount of time to see what is available in the local real estate market. They use a broker because they have neither the time nor the knowledge to follow up newspaper ads. Owners who want their homes presented to transferees should ask neighbors who were transferred in from another city as to who their broker was. This broker obviously has a number of corporate clients who have used his services for their transferred employees, and thus owners would do well to list their homes with this individual.

Another reason to use a broker is to get some protection against the merely curious, the unqualified, even the unbalanced and criminal persons who might want to tour a home for purposes that have nothing to do with a real estate transaction. The broker screens these people for his own interests as well as the seller's. Real estate agents can't afford to waste time. A broker will screen out any individual who lacks the income or downpayment to buy a house in the area or is merely desirous of going on a shopping tour.

In summary, then, the conditions under which using a broker makes good sense include the following:

- The seller has little time to deal with prospective buyers.

- A quick sale of the property is crucial.

- The local market is not particularly strong, and extensive out-of-town contacts might be necessary to find a buyer.

- The people who would ask to see the home might include unqualified individuals who should be screened out.

- The home has special features that might make it difficult to sell, a situation requiring as large a pool of potential buyers as possible.

The conditions under which one would be wise to try selling a home without a broker include these situations:

- The area is a popular one in which properties put up for sale are purchased quickly.

- The seller has enough time to write ads, prepare some basic information about the house to give prospective buyers, screen callers, and show the home.

- Most important, of course, the owner is willing to work a little harder in order to pocket the 6 to 7 percent sales commission that a broker charges for his services.

Getting The Home In Shape For Sale

NO MATTER WHETHER a home is sold by its owner or by a broker, it must be put in top condition in order to bring top dollar. A house will never bring the price that market sales of comparable property indicate it should if it appears any less than its best to prospective buyers.

What brokers call "curb appeal" is a crucially important factor. When a prospect arrives in front of the home, he or she should experience no reluctance about getting out of the car and going inside. Thus, the yard should be in good order — i.e., anything unsightly removed, shrubs and trees trimmed, the lawn mowed, and children's toys and bicycles out of sight. During winter, of course, walks should be clear of snow and ice. The buyer's immediate impression should be that this is a home that has been well maintained.

Painting the house can turn out to be a good investment if it makes a drab exterior look bright and new. On the other hand, the homeowner should only apply a neutral color (white or off-white, and this advice applies to the home's interior as well) to avoid turning off a prospect who happens not to like a particular color. The same reasoning rules against adding wallpaper or tile since the colors or materials chosen might not appeal to otherwise interested buyers.

The home's interior should look as though it has been handled carefully during the owner's residence there. A prospect who sees stains in toilets, bathtubs, and sinks quickly concludes that the people selling the home haven't taken proper care of it. Frequently, this conclusion leads to the fear that the expensive items in the

> A buyer
> will pay
> top dollar
> only for a property
> that has been
> well maintained
> and whose
> appearance reflects
> care
> and attention.

home haven't been maintained either and that big repair bills can be expected.

The owner should inspect his or her home carefully before putting it up for sale and should do all the necessary repairs and replacements that make the home show to best advantage. In this regard, he or she should keep records of every expenditure because upgrading expenses that occur within 90 days of the sale and are paid for within 30 days after the sale are deductible for income tax purposes.

Some repairs are not worthwhile making — unless they involve quite visible and serious flaws — because they probably won't return as much as they would cost to fix. For example, the roof may be nearing the end of its life. Since most prospects won't bother to check the roof carefully unless they can see some missing shingles or evidence of leaking, however, the owner would be wise merely to replace the

Preparing A Home For Sale

SELLING A HOME at the price desired is generally facilitated by putting the property in prime condition before presenting it to prospective buyers. Here is a checklist for readying the interior of the home. Homeowners should remember to keep a record of all expenses incurred 90 days before a sale and paid for within 30 days after a sale since such expenses are tax deductible.

Item   **Expense**

Windows: *Replace any broken windows, and wash all of them.*   _____

Screens: *Repair tears, holes, and other damages; replace any screens that are visibly damaged beyond repair.*   _____

Kitchen: *Replace missing or broken floor tiles and clean the ventilating hood, the top of the refrigerator, and behind the stove.*   _____

Bathrooms: *Check the caulking in the bathtubs and showers, and repair as needed; use a special cleaning compound to get rid of stains in toilets, sinks, and tubs: replace any broken tiles on the floors or walls.*   _____

Bedrooms: *Get rid of excess furniture that makes these rooms appear smaller; launder curtains and bedspreads.*   _____

Basement: *Repair any floor cracks with ready-mix concrete; paint walls a light color (preferably white) if the area is dark; remove any dank odor by turning on air conditioning or opening the windows.*   _____

Closets: *Rearrange the contents to make closets appear larger; throw out anything not really needed.*   _____

Ceilings: *Look for stains caused by leaks, and repair or repaint any problem areas; repaint any areas that are peeling.*   _____

Walls: *Replaster and repaint cracks; consider applying a light color paint on any walls that have been painted an unusual shade that some prospects might not like.*   _____

Lighting: *Replace burned-out bulbs; move existing lighting so as to eliminate dark corners; install bulbs of higher wattage to brighten the home's interior.*   _____

Plumbing: *Fix any and all faucet drips.*   _____

Heating And Cooling: *Be sure the furnace and air conditioning system work as they should, and set the thermostat to a temperature which shows prospects that the home is well heated or cooled.*   _____

Doors: *Repair any doors that stick; tighten loose knobs; scrub the front door until it looks fresh and clean.*   _____

Miscellaneous: *Clean the house thoroughly; get rid of any clutter; rearrange furniture if necessary to make rooms look larger; keep stairways clear; use ventilating equipment or open the windows to freshen the house right before a prospect is due to arrive.*   _____

missing shingles; replacing the whole roof can be an expense that will not be recovered in the sale.

On the other hand, the prospective buyer should certainly be informed of any recent improvements. For example, if the roof is just three years old, the seller or the seller's agent should make a point of mentioning it; it should, in fact, be noted on the listing card.

Helping With The Financing

TO AVOID LOSING a prospect who has everything but a downpayment, the seller should be familiar with and ready to participate in various financing arrangements. Many potential buyers would be eliminated from the housing market if they all were required to put 20 percent down in order to finance a home.

The seller should always emphasize any special financing that is available on the property. For example, the seller might be willing to offer a second mortgage to the buyer, though many lending institutions will refuse to make a first mortgage under such conditions. Certainly a seller who is willing to permit a sale under the Federal Housing Administration's mortgage insurance program or the Veterans Administration's loan guaranty program should indicate that willingness.

Normally, a seller would prefer not to offer any of these alternatives. It may be necessary, however, to sell at a time when financing a home is a problem. At such times, the seller who will make some concessions on financing will frequently find a much larger number of potential buyers and will thereby enhance the probability of a sale.

Offering a second mortgage to a prospective buyer can make sense even in good markets. The second mortgage allows the buyer to come in with a small downpayment, and a grateful buyer who would not be able to purchase the house were a full 20 percent downpayment required is not inclined to quibble over an extra few thousand dollars to be paid gradually over the next 25 years or so.

Holding a second mortgage on real estate that the seller knows to have sufficient value to cover any default can also represent an excellent investment. Consider this example:

Buyer and seller agree on a price of $60,000 for a home that originally cost $30,000. The seller has decided that with the children married and moved away, it's time to buy a smaller condominium instead of another large home. Since the condominium only costs $50,000, however, the seller is liable for capital gains taxes on the $10,000 profit acquired through the sale of the home. That liability is likely to cost at least $2,500.

To avoid the capital gains tax liability, the seller offers a $12,000 second mortgage. Since the new buyer pays that sum in monthly installments instead of in a lump sum, only a small portion of the profit is immediately taxable. Eventually the seller will face a tax liability, but meanwhile he or she will enjoy the benefit of an excellent return on invested capital as well as, most likely, top dollar on the sale of the house.

The buyer also benefits in this situation. He or she can finance the remaining $48,000 with a conventional 80 percent mortgage and make no downpayment whatsoever on the new purchase. The monthly payments will be steep, but since none of the buyer's own money is tied up in the property, any value appreciation returns almost 100 percent profit.

The risks of a second mortgage to the seller are not significant so long as the value of the property is maintained or increases. Should the buyer fail to make payments on the first mortgage, that lender will either foreclose and sell the property or take title to it in order to get his money back. A sale should produce enough cash to pay off the second mortgage as well, assuming that the home goes at market value. If the first mortgage holder merely takes possession without attempting to sell — a rare occurrence — the second mortgage holder would also be paid off.

The second mortgage holder can assure repayment by initiating foreclosure when the present owner fails to make payments instead of waiting for the first mortgage holder to do so.

By foreclosing on the second mortgage first (possible even if it is the first mortgage holder who is not being paid), the second mortgage lender can take over the property, continue the monthly payments to the first mortgage holder, and conduct a sale of the home which guarantees that both parties will get their money back.

For assuming these minimal risks, moreover, the second mortgage lender usually earns at least 10 percent interest and frequently even more than that.

Government-backed loans are not nearly so attractive to the seller. Though FHA and VA loans allow many more people to buy because the interest rates and downpayment requirements are lower than with conventional mortgages, the lender who handles the transaction charges several points — usually 2 to 5 percent of the loan — to compensate for the lower interest rate. Since government regulations prohibit the home buyer from paying this fee, the points charges come out of the seller's pocket.

It frequently does little good to price a home higher in order to recover the points fee involved in a government-backed loan. FHA and VA appraisers make their own estimates of the value of the home, and although FHA buyers are permitted to pay the difference between the sale price and the FHA appraisal in cash, VA buyers are not.

Another drawback for the seller who agrees to a government-backed loan is that the paperwork can take a long time to process. It may take four weeks before an FHA or VA appraiser comes out to look at the property, and another two weeks can go by before a decision is reached on what the government will agree to insure. Therefore, any seller who thinks that an FHA or VA loan might be involved in the purchase of the property should start the process moving several weeks before putting the home on the market.

Private mortgage insurance represents yet another way that a seller can help a prospect who lacks sufficient capital for the downpayment. Better than government-insured loans in that it doesn't cost the seller anything,

> A seller can help a potential buyer surmount the downpayment hurdle via several special financing arrangements.

private mortgage insurance is not as attractive to a buyer because it actually pushes the interest rate higher by 0.25 percent and because it involves a conventional mortgage which is typically 0.50 percent higher than an FHA or VA mortgage.

Here is how private mortgage insurance works. One of the several large national mortgage insurance companies (lenders can supply names of reliable firms) agrees to insure the top 10 percent of a loan that covers 90 percent of the value of the house. The lender thus takes the standard risk of making an 80 percent mortgage, offering the borrower an additional 10 percent that is guaranteed by the private insurer. As a consequence, the buyer must come up with a downpayment of just 10 percent.

The typical fee for this service is 0.25 percent of the outstanding principal. In other words, instead of the buyer paying 8.75 percent on 80 percent of the purchase, he or she pays 9 percent on 90 percent, with the extra quarter point going to the private insurer. Although it is an expensive alternative to regular financing, sellers should suggest private mortgage insurance to buyers who lack the capital for a standard downpayment.

Finally, there is the contract sale in which the buyer never really holds the deed to the property until he or she either pays off the purchase price to the seller in monthly sums or arranges financing that pays it in full. A contract sale can be useful to a seller seeking to defer a profit while also continuing to receive tax deductions for interest payments on an existing mortgage. It makes sense, for example, for the seller who plans to rent his or her next residence to retain possession of the home and continue to make mortgage payments on it while receiving monthly payments from the buyer according to the terms of a written contract between the two parties. When the buyer's payments reach the point at which they represent a satisfactory downpayment (usually five to seven years), the contract is terminated and the seller receives all the money due from the sale of the home from the buyer's mortgage lender.

Due to the complexity of a contract sale, it is important to consult an attorney before drawing up the document. A contract sale is quite safe, however, since the property owner never loses title rights to the home until receiving full payment. It can also be beneficial to a buyer who wants the seller's home but cannot come up with a sufficient downpayment to receive a standard mortgage loan.

Assuming Or Taking Over A Mortgage

ONE FINAL NOTE about financing from the seller's viewpoint: It is possible for a buyer to assume the loan payment obligations of a seller if the seller's mortgage does not prohibit a transfer of the property subject to the mortgage. However, one should have an attorney's advice on such assumption and how best to limit a seller's continuing liability on the original loan. All FHA and VA mortgages are assumable, for example, and many conventional mortgages written before the mid 1960's often contain the clause allowing a transfer of the property to another person subject to the debt obligation.

Sellers who do possess such mortgages need not even inform the government or the lender before transferring their debt obligations.

Depending on the terms of the seller, the seller will retain a certain measure of liability for the debt. Since the value of the home in most cases greatly exceeds the remaining principle, however, the seller really faces very little risk. If the person who takes over the loan payments defaults, the original owner has the right to force a foreclosure on the property, if necessary, to have the debt paid.

The interest rates on these mortgages are usually so low by today's standards that potential buyers will go to great lengths to purchase a home with a loan that can be taken over. They will do their best to come up with enough downpayment or with a second mortgage in order to take over the remaining debt at that low rate. Therefore, a mortgage that can be assumed or taken over is a major sales tool that almost guarantees the seller of getting top dollar for the property. Any home investor would be delighted to pay just 6 percent, for example, on a good piece of residential real estate that might well be appreciating in value at twice that rate.

A broker frequently counsels both buyer and seller about all the financing options open to them, and occasionally this information that the broker provides is crucial to making a sale. An owner selling his or her own home, therefore, would be wise to learn about financing alternatives and be ready to explain to potential buyers how each one operates.

Sellers who can offer
an assumable mortgage
at a low interest rate
possess a
potent sales tool.

Profits And Taxes

UPON SELLING THE home, the investor receives the full profit that a wise purchase and proper maintenance guaranteed. That profit is subject to a capital gains tax, although the government extends special tax treatment to people who sell and then buy another home within a year and a half. So long as the home was the seller's principal residence and he or she buys another home of equal or greater value as a principal residence within 18 months (24 months if the seller builds a new home), the government does not tax the seller's profit. Should the seller not intend to invest the profit received from selling a home in another home, then he or she must be prepared to pay a capital gains tax, which usually means that about 25 percent of the profit goes to the government.

Sellers who intend to take advantage of the government's special treatment should report their intentions to the IRS in the year of the sale by filing Form 2119 with their regular income tax return. If a seller were then to fail to purchase a home of higher value in 18 or 24 months, the IRS would charge a penalty of 7 percent interest on the capital gains tax liability; both the tax and the penalty, of course, would be payable immediately.

It should be emphasized that a seller cannot avoid the capital gains tax by using the profits from the sale of a principal residence to buy investment real estate. Similarly, the profits earned on the sale of investment real estate cannot be deferred by reinvesting them in a principal place of residence.

A smart seller, however, can utilize the IRS provisions to take a cash profit out of a sale without paying taxes on it. He or she merely buys another principal residence of equal or greater value and mortgages the new property to the full 80 percent. The difference between the new 20 percent downpayment and the total profit on the old home (after paying off the old mortgage) goes to the seller with no immediate tax.

For example, the investor sells a residence for $60,000, making $30,000 over the initial price of the home. Then the investor buys a condominium for the same $60,000 price, paying $12,000 down on an 80 percent mortgage. The difference between the $30,000 profit and

the $12,000 downpayment — $18,000 — escapes federal income tax until (if ever) the investor disposes of the condominium and does not replace it with another residence of equal or higher value.

The seller who finally does pay a capital gains tax on the profit should be aware that the cost of major improvements made to the property are tax deductible. Installing air conditioning or finishing a basement or an attic during the time that the seller holds the property is considered a capital improvement, and if the seller has records to prove these expenses were incurred, he or she should be certain to deduct the expenditures from the profit.

Elderly people (i.e., those over age 65) receive an additional tax break in that any profit on the first $35,000 of the home's sale price is exempt from the capital gains liability. The IRS rule stipulates, however, that the seller must have lived in the residence for at least five of the previous eight years to qualify.

Suppose that an elderly seller has lived in a home for 25 years after purchasing the property for $15,000. Today, the home is worth $45,000. A seller under age 65 would incur a capital gains tax on $30,000 by not replacing that property with something at least as expensive within 18 or 24 months. But the elderly seller in this example would not be subject to tax on the first $35,000 of the home's $45,000 sale price.

The 1976 Tax Reform Act included a provision known as the minimum tax on capital gains. This provision applies only to sellers who do not replace their homes with residences equally expensive or more so. It says that half of the capital gain — less $10,000 (instead of the previous $30,000) — is subject to a 15 percent minimum tax.

An example will illustrate how this rule works. Assume a home is sold for $60,000; it originally cost $20,000, and the seller put $5,000 into capital improvements. The profit, therefore, amounts to $60,000 minus $25,000, or $35,000. Half of that amount is subject to the full capital gains tax. The other half, $17,500, is subject to the 15 percent minimum tax as specified in the 1976 Tax Reform Act. Since the provision al-

Home sellers can receive preferential tax treatment on the profit derived from the sale.

lows for a $10,000 exemption, however, the 15 percent tax applies only to $7,500, resulting in a tax liability of $1,125.

How To Profit By Selling

IN SUMMARY, then, anyone can sell a home for maximum profit; it's all a matter of handling the following sales factors correctly.

- Watch for the onset of worsening economic conditions or a tight money situation that will reduce the number of potential buyers; sell right before these factors influence the home market.

- Determine whether a broker's services are required.

- Do everything possible to avoid the double-mortgage squeeze.

- Price the home slightly above market value.

- Put the house in first-class condition for showing.

- Offer special financing to prospects who need assistance and who are willing to pay top dollar for the home.

- Take full advantage of the preferential tax treatment the government extends to home-owners.

Part II:

BiG AL
YOUR FRIENDLY PLUMBER
601-5678

HANDY HAR HOME REMODELE

Sundi's INTERIOR DECORATING

Maintaining And Improving The Home For

Profit

Maintaining And Improving The Home For Profit

ARTHUR JACKSON immediately liked two things about a home he was shown while house-hunting back in 1969. First, the property was only a short block from much more expensive homes. Second, it was priced about $2,000 less than houses on the same block because it was the only one without a finished basement. By finishing the basement, Jackson realized he could put this home on a par with the adjoining properties.

Jackson was correct in his assessment of the investment potential of the property. Sub-standard homes are helped by their proximity to more expensive housing, and improvements that place them on equal footing with the more costly homes are always good investments.

Because he could perform some rudimentary carpentry, moreover, Jackson figured that he could do much of the work necessary to finish the basement by himself. He also knew a retired carpenter who liked to do small jobs to stay active and who would supply the needed skills when the project was beyond Jackson's own abilities.

Finishing the basement took about two years of spare-time construction work. The carpenter, who charged only $7 an hour (well below the union scale), quickly got interested in seeing that the project was done right, and he gave Jackson plenty of free instruction.

"I made about $20,000 on that house in six years," Jackson said after selling it in 1975. "That basement knocked people's eyes out; it had to mean $8,000 to the eventual sale price. And since I spent only a couple of thousand to produce it, I figure it paid for itself three or four times over — not to mention the pleasure we got from entertaining down there."

Jackson's experience illustrates that some home improvements do pay for themselves. They must really make a contribution to the living area and to the convenience of a home, and they must be done well but at a low cost.

To realize the greatest return on a home investment, the investor should make his or her home comparable to other homes in the neighborhood but not spend so much as to make it much better than adjoining property. Buyers won't pay for what real estate pros call an "over-improvement." Producing a dazzling garden, for example, doesn't pay off in most cases. In fact, a spectacular garden limits the number of people who might buy the home to those who have the time or inclination to maintain the shrubs and flowers.

What the home investor's goal should be is to enjoy the property to the fullest during the period he or she resides there, but to do so at minimum out-of-pocket cost. The necessary improvements that add to comfort and/or reduce expenses — such as in-

> Improvements
> should make
> a home
> equal to —
> but not
> much better
> than — surrounding
> properties.

sulation — should be made as soon as possible after the home is purchased. Not only will the home investor benefit from such improvements for the whole period of occupancy, but also the appreciation in value usually will make any improvement pay for itself when the house goes on the market if sufficient time has elapsed since the cost of the improvement was incurred.

Suppose a new homeowner spends $5,000 to remodel an outdated kitchen. If he or she sells the home within a year or two of the remodelling job, it is highly unlikely that the full $5,000 expenditure will be recovered. Over a five-year period, however, the price of the home will probably escalate to such an extent that all improvements initially made on the property will be recovered. If the homeowner were to try to sell the home with the outdated kitchen, moreover, the price that he or she could get would probably be lower by at least the $5,000 it would have taken to modernize the kitchen right from the start.

"Don't expect the value of your house to go up the exact amount that you put into home improvements," warns Robert G. Walters, senior vice president of the Chicago-based real estate firm of Baird & Warner. "It is still more expensive to modernize an existing house than for a builder to put those features into a new house. When you're remodelling, you're cutting into floors and walls. You have to tear down before you build up, and all that construction raises the price of your work."

Walters suggests looking at the most expensive house on your street. "Try to find out what that house has that makes it more costly than others around it. If it has two or three bathrooms with all the latest plumbing features, then maybe it's worth it to plunge into that particular addition. But remember, don't price yourself out of the market."

As a general rule, a new or greatly modernized kitchen, an additional bathroom, a finished family room, or an extra bedroom will return from 50 to 75 percent of its cost if the home is sold within a year or two. The idea, then, is to make improvements that — in addition to making the home a more pleasant place to live in — will pay for themselves in the home's overall appreciation over several years.

Modernizing And Adding To The Home

Maintaining And Improving The Home For Profit

THE BEST IMPROVEMENTS, from an investment standpoint, are the most visible ones. In other words, new plumbing fixtures count for more than new pipes, and new lighting fixtures return more than new electrical wiring. The exterior of the home should look well maintained because it gives the first and last impression to a prospective buyer; peeling paint and missing roof shingles almost invariably prove costly on resale. An attractive yard is important, although elaborate landscaping seldom contributes to the sale price.

In some areas of the country, the addition of a garage can be an excellent investment. In others, central air conditioning will almost always pay for itself in added value. It is, crucial, therefore, to evaluate what is expected in a home within a certain locale (or even in a particular neighborhood) before spending any money on additions or improvements.

Investors should strive to bring a substandard home up to the level of other nearby homes. For example, adding central air conditioning to a home in close proximity to centrally air conditioned houses usually raises the formerly sub-standard home to equal footing with its neighbors. Thus, a house that sells for $3,000 less than others in the neighborhood because it lacks air conditioning might well jump that much in value immediately following a $2,000 investment in a central cooling system.

To make the most of a home improvement, the investor wants to combine all the factors that generate profits and reduce costs while simultaneously enhancing personal living comfort. If central air conditioning reduces utility costs by eliminating the use of several room air conditioners, it thereby becomes an improvement that pays double dividends. Similarly, a garage that prolongs the life of a car and reduces maintenance costs is the type of addition that smart home investors would not ignore.

The improvements that consistently pay off best on resale are those that add to or upgrade the fundamental living areas. Adding a patio, swimming pool, or even a recreation room, therefore, is questionable in terms of return on investment. All are expensive additions to make, they don't appeal to everybody, and they can be costly and/or time-consuming to maintain.

"Addition of a basement recreation room is an 'iffy' improvement," says Robert G. Walters of the Baird & Warner real estate company. "Times have definitely changed over the last 10 or 20 years. Teenagers and adults use outside recreational facilities more and don't use their homes or basements for entertaining in the same way they did years ago. A tiled and panelled recreation room and bar may be heaven to you, but it could be viewed as just a relic of the past by future buyers."

Good landscaping (but not too good) generally represents an investment that is easy to recover. In fact, some home advisers say one of the best financial commitments an owner can make is to plant a tree, especially one that shields a house from direct sunlight. The planting of deciduous trees on the major sun wall of a home provides shade in the summer yet lets the winter sun in after the leaves fall. A well-maintained lawn can be profitable, especially in suburban areas.

Determining And Controlling Improvement Costs

WHAT ABOUT the costs of home improvements? Here are some estimates by one prominent national savings and loan association:

- Bathroom remodelling, $3,000
- Kitchen remodelling, $4,000
- Porch enclosure, $2,500
- New gutters, $450
- New roof, $1,100
- Aluminum screens and storm windows, $600
- Sidewall insulation, $800

These figures are based on the property owner employing professional help, and the costs would certainly be substantially lower were the homeowner to do some or all of the labor him or herself.

Chicago real estate appraiser Charles A.

Benson points out that "an improvement job might not be translated into value unless the owner puts his own labor into it. Eventual profit depends a lot on whether you can do it yourself or must have a contractor do it. If you do it yourself, you stand a better chance of recovering the costs of the improvement."

Anything you can do yourself figures to be more easily recovered because you are paying no costs for labor, only for materials. But it's important that any improvement or addition look like professional work. One real estate expert warns, "Unless you're a competent tradesperson, don't tackle the improvement job on your own. You may be trying to save money, but instead may wind up with a botched-up job that will either cost you money to redo or even lower your price at resale time."

What a home investor wants to avoid when improving property is paying the going rate for skilled labor. Some tradesmen charge as much as $20 an hour, and, therefore, having professionals do all or a substantial part of an improvement may make the project not worthwhile from an investment standpoint. In order to receive the dollars previously spent on improvements at the time of resale, the homeowner must produce those improvements inexpensively.

What options are open to the homeowner contemplating an improvement but reluctant to pay the prevailing labor rate? He or she should talk to the maintenance engineer in a nearby apartment building; these people often have plumbing and carpentry skills. An advertisement in the classified section of the newspaper can also result in finding someone with the requisite skills who won't charge the top union wage.

The homeowner should turn to a contractor for remodelling or adding a room only as a last resort. And before selecting a specific contractor, the property owner should get answers to some very important questions. Does the contractor maintain liability insurance on his own employees and on any sub-contractors who work for him? Will he arrange for all permits and inspections and be responsible for their cost?

Will he provide a warranty on the work done? All of these questions should be answered affirmatively before the homeowner signs any contract.

Since contractors perform better when they know exactly what is desired, the wise owner develops as specific a description as possible of the work to be done. This should be a written description, and it should include the specific types of materials to be used.

In choosing materials, a smart investor resists anything exceptionally expensive or fancy. The very best wood panelling or fixtures or tile may be aesthetically pleasing, but none will come close to returning its cost when the home is sold.

The owner who goes the contractor route should be sure of actually obtaining high quality work performed by a reputable company. By deciding in advance exactly what work is to be done and what materials are to be used, the owner can then get estimates from three contractors whose work is well known in the community. Of course, seeing examples of each contractor's previous work is the best approach to take.

A contractor files a report on what work he has been hired to do when he requests a building permit for any substantial improvement or addition — such as remodelling a bathroom. Since the report could very well bring a building inspector out to see that the work is done in compliance with the city building code, the homeowner should have a contract that specifies that all work must meet local building code regulations. Such a provision gives the homeowner a legal basis for requiring the contractor to make necessary adjustments if the job fails to comply.

The contractor's report could also bring an appraiser from the assessor's office to reappraise the property and usually increase the amount of its assessed value due to the improvement or addition. Most reappraisals, though, actually result in no more than a minor increase in the property tax unless the improvement is quite elaborate — like the addition of a room or a two-car garage.

Maintaining And Improving The Home For Profit

In the end, whether or not to spend money for a home improvement depends on these factors:

1. The length of time between the improvement and the sale of the property. Owners who hold the property for less than three years after making an improvement seldom recover their costs.

2. What the improvement will do to the property in comparison with other homes in the neighborhood. If the improvement brings a home up to neighborhood standards, the expenditure probably makes sense. If the improvement places a home way above other residences in the area, however, the chances for recovering the cost of the improvement at resale is much less likely.

3. The degree to which potential buyers recognize and appreciate the improvement. Unless the improvement is recognizable and appreciated, it may not be worth doing.

4. The amount of work that the property owner can do him or herself to cut professional labor costs.

How To Finance Home Improvements

FINDING MONEY to finance home improvements generally represents no real problem. Banks and savings associations both like to make home improvement loans, usually charging about three percent above their rates for home mortgages. A credit union may be an even better source, charging interest rates a couple of percentage points below the bank rate. Borrowing against a life insurance policy or a savings account can also result in paying a lower interest rate.

A program of the federal government called "HUD-insured Title I Home Improvement Loans" provides one of the easiest ways to get low-interest money for making home improvements. Depending on the nature of the improvement, a borrower can obtain up to $10,000 at an interest rate that usually is two percentage points below the conventional rate. Repairs, alterations, or improvements that substantially protect or improve the basic living quality or utility of a home qualify for the full $10,000 loan, with a 12-year period to pay it off. For a larger dwelling (one housing two or more families) the limit of the HUD-insured loans is $5,000 per unit.

Homeowners should be sure to ask a lending institution how the lender's own plan compares to the HUD plan. Most lenders offer both types of loans, but they typically charge more for their own plans because such loans are not insured like the federally backed improvement funds. On the other hand, they often sweeten their plans by allowing a 15-year payback period and a $15,000 ceiling as opposed to HUD's 12-year plan and $10,000 limit. The property owner can initiate either type of loan through the lending institution; HUD-insured loans are not obtained directly from the federal government.

An owner seeking home improvement financing should also check the open-end provisions of his or her mortgage. Under the open-end provision, accumulated equity may be added back to the mortgage in the form of an addition to the loan. For example, a $30,000 mortgage paid down to $26,000 can be raised back to the original $30,000, with the $4,000 difference going to the homeowner in cash for the needed improvement. Since the interest rate for the entire $30,000 mortgage will jump to the current percentage, however, exercising the open-end provision may or may not be advantageous. A second mortgage for the amount needed to finance a home improvement might be less expensive than paying a higher rate of interest on the entire original loan.

> Home improvement loans are readily available from a variety of sources.

One of the best plans for home improvement financing is to take out a second mortgage with a balloon payment of the principal. The homeowner pays only the interest charges for five to eight years until the principal comes due. By that time, the owner may well have sold the house after realizing the benefits of the improvement during ownership and the profits the improvement brings at resale. The interest payments, of course, provide a tax deduction during the ownership period, and money for the balloon payment can be taken from the proceeds of the sale.

Speaking of tax advantages, the cost of home improvements can and should be deducted from the eventual profit at sale. Thus, a $20,000 profit on a home on which $5,000 in improvements have been made means that the seller is responsible for a capital gain of just $15,000. It is essential, therefore, to keep complete records of all improvement expenses during the entire period of ownership.

Controlling Heating And Cooling Costs

Maintaining And Improving The Home For Profit

THE PRIMARY maintenance expenses that a homeowner faces relate to keeping a home warm during winter and cool during summer. Naturally, the extent to which an owner can reduce these expenses through energy-saving techniques will lead to a greater degree of profitability from the residence.

"Tightening up" a home represents a modest expense that can pay big dividends during both the period of occupancy and at resale. The homeowner can do much of the work by installing some simple and inexpensive devices to cut the cost of heating and cooling, and generally recover the total improvement expenditure through reduced utility bills in a period of five to seven years. In addition, an owner marketing a home that has been tightened up possesses an excellent selling point at resale time.

Here are some relatively inexpensive ways to tighten up a home.

1. Add storm windows. Storm windows prevent the loss of heated air during winter and the loss of cooled air during summer. Components are available at lumber yards and hardware stores that allow homeowners to make storm windows for nearly every situation, even for odd-sized windows. The components are easy to assemble, and they save about 15 to 20 percent over having the units made professionally.

2. Install window shades. Window shades can also protect against significant energy loss. In one study by the Illinois Institute of Technology, a drawn roller shade prevented 24 to 31 percent of the heat loss that normally occurred through glass in winter, and it admitted 54 percent less heat during summer than an unshaded window.

3. Apply solar screening (available at hardware stores and lumber yards) to windows. Solar screening's main benefits occur during summer when it can block as much as 75 percent of the sun's heat by reflecting the rays. This heat, therefore, never reaches the interior of the room, where it would cause the air conditioning system to work harder.

4. Attach weatherstripping around windows and doors, including interior doors that lead to unheated attics, basements, or other areas. Utility companies have estimated that air seeping through cracks around windows and doors can account for as much heat loss as would occur through a three-foot hole in the wall.

5. Apply caulking around windows, doors, and the openings for pipes and wires that enter a home. A modest investment in a caulking gun and caulking material almost always comes back in fuel savings.

6. Replace an old thermostat with a timer-controlled unit that automatically lowers the level of heat or air conditioning at night and raises it the following morning. These thermostats can save a great deal of energy, thereby reducing heating and cooling costs considerably. Tests have shown that a night timer setback of 10 degrees

---

Improvements that save energy pay off in lower utility bills and higher resale prices.

can save from 9 to 15 percent on heating costs, depending upon the area. Of course, manually setting the thermostat every night will achieve the same result, but the automatic timer makes certain that the setback occurs every night and that the home will be comfortably heated or cooled by the time the occupants get up every morning.

7. Add a heat pump. Heat pumps can return their purchase price in reduced heating costs because they extract warmth from outside air and pump it into the home during winter. When the weather outside is warm, the heat pump reverses its function, pumping the hot air inside the home out and blowing cool air in. Any homeowner who intends to stay in a home for a reasonably long period of time should investigate the costs and projected savings of having a heat pump installed.

8. Run a humidifier during the heating season. A humidifier makes the air feel up to five degrees warmer, allowing the thermostat to be dialed to a lower setting. It also makes the home a more comfortable place in which to live.

9. Run an attic ventilating fan during the cooling season. An attic fan that expels hot air during the summer consumes only a small amount of energy compared to what it saves in the electricity needed to run the air conditioning system. Some attic fans have thermostatic controls, and there are even wind-operated units that require no electricity whatsoever.

Insulating A Home

IN CONTRAST to the above do-it-yourself energy-saving projects, the task of fully insulating a home may require an insulation contractor. Generally, a homeowner can insulate an attic floor without calling in outside help and incurring a labor cost, but more extensive appli-

> Installing
> adequate
> insulation
> is equivalent
> to putting money
> in the bank.

cations of insulating material usually require a professional's services. That means getting bids from three companies that specialize in the field, and checking their past work and reputations. It pays to be careful about who does the work because a number of dishonest insulation operators sprang up after the winter of 1976-77, trying to make big money out of the sudden demand for insulation without providing commensurate quality in either materials or workmanship.

If a homeowner must turn to an insulation contractor, he or she should exercise great care in selecting a firm to do the work and should ask for a certificate of performance stating that the installation will meet specifications. If the job is not done right, this certificate can be used to get an adjustment. Reputable contractors will provide such a certificate, one of the few protections a consumer has in an area where few installation standards have been set by law.

A homeowner should strive to end up with attic insulation amounting to an R-value of 19 to 30, and wall insulation with an R-value of 11 to 16. R-value refers to the insulating material's resistance to heat transfer, and the resistance

Energy-Saver's Checklist

A HOMEOWNER can do a great many things to save energy — and thereby reduce utility bills — that require no expenditure whatsoever. Here is a checklist of some of them.

Close off unoccupied rooms and shut off the heating or air conditioning to them.

Lower the thermostat five to ten degrees at night during the heating season.

Keep windows near the thermostat closed so that they won't affect the operation of the heating/cooling system.

When using the fireplace, reduce the thermostat setting to minimize heat waste.

Keep the fireplace damper closed except when a fire is burning to prevent heat loss.

Clean or replace the filters in a forced-air heating system once a month; do the same for a central air conditioning system.

Dust or vacuum radiator surfaces regularly to prevent dirt from impeding heat flow.

Open draperies and shades on sunny windows during winter days and close them at night.

Close draperies and shades on sunny windows during summer.

Reduce the temperature setting on the water heater from high to medium.

Turn off the water heater when you go on vacation.

Do household cleaning with cold water.

Set the wash cycle on a washing machine for warm or cold water and the rinse cycle for cold water.

Take showers instead of tub baths.

Fill dishwashers and washing machines before running them (but don't overload them).

Clean the lint screen and outside exhaust of a clothes dryer regularly.

Don't let frost build up more than a quarter inch before defrosting a freezer.

Turn off lights, especially during summer when the extra heat generated is not wanted.

Replace light bulbs with ones of lower wattage, and keep all bulbs free of dust.

Use ventilating fans sparingly because they rob the house of warm or cool air.

figure is listed on insulating material. R-3, for example, corresponds to approximately a one-inch thickness of glass fiber insulating material.

The attic is the best place to add insulation because the attic is where most of a home's heat escapes. The typical home with poor insulation — older homes usually have only three inches of attic insulation — can lose up to 40 percent of its total heat through the attic. By adding six inches of insulation, the homeowner can often cut his or her heat loss down to about 15 percent.

Suppose, for example, an owner decides to upgrade the insulation in his 1,400 square foot home to R-22. The insulating material costs about $420, to which he adds two storm doors at $75 each, 12 triple-track storm windows at $30 each, and $10 worth of caulking supplies. The total improvement costs $940, but the resulting savings in energy amounts to about $230 a year; thus, in a little more than four years the homeowner will recover out-of-pocket costs spent to tighten up the home.

"Assuming a 20-year life for the improvements, the original $940 investment would return $3,660," points out John Domeier, president of Great American Federal Savings and Loan Association in Chicago. "That's a good return in anyone's language." And, of course, the return will be even better if energy costs continue to rise at anything like the pace of the mid-1970's.

Naturally, smart home investors try to buy homes that need little or no extra attention to insulation, seeking residences in which someone else has already taken on the expense of insulation. There are some easy ways to test whether a property in question is properly insulated. One is to hold a thermometer near the floor and compare the temperature there with the setting of the thermostat. If the floor temperature is several degrees lower, then heat is escaping and the house probably needs additional insulation.

Simply touching the walls to see how cold they are is another good test. Walls that are adequately insulated should not be cold to the touch. Heat loss through the attic is often re-vealed by snow on the roof melting more rapidly than it does on other houses. The faster the snow melts, the greater the heat loss.

How much insulating the homeowner can do for him or herself depends on an individual willingness to spend time installing either rolled blanket or loose-fill insulation; both materials constitute a rather simple installation in an attic floor. Most homeowners put in either fiberglass or rock wool, either of which can provide sufficient R-value. It is very important that any material used for insulating purposes should be fire retardant, moisture resistant, and insect and rodent proof — and should so state on the label.

According to Donald Jedele, University of Illinois Cooperative Extension housing specialist, homeowners are often ignorant of the best ways to insulate. He points to one particular problem when installing loose-fill material in an attic. "Pouring wool is packed so tightly into a paper bag that when you cut the bag open, you still have a solid lump of compressed insulation. That lump has to be fluffed up and spread around. If there is adequate head room in your attic, make a platform where you can

Smart home
shoppers
look for signs
of energy
efficiency
before buying.

open the bags and break up the mineral wool. You can then rake it to the low corners at the eaves.''

Jedele also recommends that consumers not be taken in by advertising claims regarding the energy-saving effects of batt insulation with aluminum foil facing. "Some advertising might cause people to think that aluminum foil reflects heat and therefore works best. But the bright aluminum surface cannot reflect heat unless there is at least a ¾-inch air space between the foil and the wall or ceiling line. In this day of full-thick wall batts and 6- to 12-inch ceiling in-

sulation, there cannot be a ¾-inch air space, so no heat is reflected by the foil."

Installing wall insulation is much more difficult for the do-it-yourselfer, though it is possible to rent a machine to blow the foam-like insulation material into walls. The machine blows foam between the interior and exterior walls where it hardens into a plastic-like substance. But poor mixing when the foam is fluid can cause water and odor problems, and since the foam shrinks over time, it takes someone with knowledge of the substance to handle this kind of installation properly.

Some walls must be insulated from the inside. By applying thin furring strips, insulating between them, and covering the wall with paneling, the homeowner can achieve results comparable to insulation blown in from the outside. The process is expensive, however, and it seldom pays for itself.

Insulating the underside of the house — especially an unfinished basement or crawl space — may be worthwhile for the homeowner who expects to keep the house for more than five years. Heated basements need wall insulation, while unheated basements need ceiling insulation to protect the living area above. The heat loss through these spaces, though, may not justify the expenditure.

According to a study by the National Bureau of Standards, the payback periods for insulation in walls, ceilings, and floors ranged from 9.5 to 17.5 years, depending on climate, efficiency of the furnace, cost of fuel, and structure of the house. Interestingly, the payback period for storm windows was just 5.4 to 10.2 years (again depending on the type of heating plant, etc.), making storm windows an even more attractive investment for the energy-conscious homeowner.

Before making any investment in supplementary insulation, the wise homeowner will do some research, trying to find what difference additional insulation is likely to make in future heating and cooling costs. Often, the utility companies can give the homeowner a percentage figure as to the annual savings from full or partial insulation. Then, it's merely a matter of figuring out how long it will take to recover the investment. Of course, additional insulation also boosts the value of the home (the utility companies may have some estimates on that amount, too), and smart homeowners use "before and after" heating and cooling bills to good advantage when showing a recently insulated home to potential buyers.

Builders definitely believe in using insulation as a selling point in the marketing of new homes. Recent surveys by *Professional Builder* magazine into the experience of many builders indicate that buyers usually will take an

Home sellers can use their homes' good insulation as a strong selling point.

energy-saving package if it is offered as an extra-cost item in a new home. The surveys show quite clearly that today's buyers are energy-conscious and are willing to pay more in purchase price to reduce their monthly operating expenses over the long term.

Part III: What

TWO BUYERS who invest the same amount of money in a home on the same day in the same community could five years later find that one owns a property worth twice as much as the other. The eventual profit from a home depends that much on the type of property chosen, in what neighborhood or school district it is, and other factors affecting the city where it is located.

Consider two different types of investment, both having the potential of great profitability.

In the first situation, a new subdivision has been announced for an urban area already established as a prime residential

Should You Buy?

neighborhood for people in the middle to upper-middle income range. The white-collar population of the city has been growing strongly for several years, and this particular area has become increasingly popular with that group. In addition, the builder of this new subdivision has already built homes in the area that have shown good appreciation on resale.

Now, the builder announces a pre-opening sale; prices are lower than those that will be offered after the units are completed six months to two years later. The prices are higher than they were in the last subdivision built in the area by the same contractor but lower than those of existing homes where the landscaping has been developed and homeowner improvements

Buy
a new home
early, preferably
during
a builder's
pre-opening
sale.

have been made. Buying so early, the investor can only see floor plans of the house; but, by driving around the area, he or she can observe what the builder's other houses are like and perhaps get opinions about them from some of the owners.

Builders lower prices only in dire economic circumstances. They are locked into higher wages for skilled labor, higher materials costs, and higher land costs. They must price a new home to cover these costs; but builders often want to assure themselves that they will have some money coming in early. Therefore, they frequently hold pre-opening sales with prices appealingly lower than will be the case when the units are there to see.

It is, of course, risky to buy anything sight unseen, but a builder of tract housing usually builds the same models over and over. The potential buyer should first ask how different the new units will be compared to those in the builder's other subdivisions, and then go out and examine the earlier subdivisions. Later, he or she can inquire at a local savings and loan association about resales in those subdivisions. Builders quickly gain a reputation for the quality of the homes they build and the way that quality is reflected on resale. An appraiser at a savings and loan association generally knows about home builders and prices in the area, and he can usually supply proof of what he knows for a small fee ($100 to $150 typically).

For maximum profit, the pre-opening sale is the time to buy a home in a subdivision with promise. Within a year, these homes figure to be more expensive by at least the annual inflation rate. More importantly, the demand will increase sharply when model homes are open and the public can actually see what the finished homes look like.

In the second case of great potential profitability, the investor is looking at a neighborhood that had been slipping steadily into decline but in which renovation activity is becoming apparent. The location is very good for transportation, schools, and social activities. The homes, however, had not been well maintained during the past few years, and in many cases they had been sold to absentee owners who converted them into rental buildings, dividing the space to acquire more income.

A talk with a broker who handles property in the area indicates that several properties have recently been sold to people who have begun to renovate them for their own homes. Prices are already rising in response to this buyer interest; in fact, they have climbed 20 percent in the last year. A visit with a savings and loan appraiser who knows the area reveals that in most cases the homes are structurally sound and that renovation is definitely feasible.

What remains now is to select one of these properties, talk to a broker about it, and determine what he can do about interesting the owner in selling it. After that is accomplished and a favorable engineering report on the building is obtained, the investor seeking a maximum profit should try to make a deal. The property is probably as cheap as it ever will be. Soon other investors will note that this neighborhood is quickly changing for the better, and the demand then will be so strong that one would not be able to buy the property in question at anything like the present market value.

These two examples illustrate several important considerations about what and where to buy. Basically, the smart profit-oriented buyer looks for the growth area of a city, especially an area that middle-income people can afford. There are more buyers in this class, and they tend to put more effort into improving and upgrading

their homes.

One cautionary note, however: Make certain that the area has begun to stabilize before investing there. If it is still too early to tell whether a new area can handle a large and sudden population growth, be wary. If, however, the school system is absorbing newcomers without ill effects, the water and sewer problems are minimal, the local government still favors growth instead of trying to shut it off, and the early homes built there are worth substantially more today than when they were first constructed, the investment risks are minimal, and the smart home buyer does not hesitate to purchase potentially profitable property there.

Single-Family Homes

Vs. Other Types Of Investment Property

What Should You Buy?

VIRGINIA MOORE thinks the best property to buy for investment is a condominium near downtown Chicago. That is because she is single, doesn't pretend or want to be handy, can't stand such chores as lawn mowing, and wants to be near the good restaurants and social centers of a high-class urban neighborhood. For Virginia Moore, the purchase of a condominium is the correct investment.

Condominium values were slow to increase until about 1976. By then, however, the concept had been around long enough so that most people felt comfortable about condominium investment. New consumer protection laws added to the confidence of potential condominium buyers, and suddenly there was a strong market for new, converted (from rental), and existing condominium units.

At present, the typical condominium in a well-located area shows just a bit less annual appreciation than a comparable single-family house. The condominium, however, generally costs less per square foot than the home because land costs are significantly less; if the condominium is in a high-rise building, moreover, the construction costs are lower than those for a comparable house.

On the other hand, Robert Morris — another home investor — thinks Virginia Moore's concept of a good home investment is not good at all. He can point to objective surveys that show that the dream home of 94 percent of the American people is a single-family house on its own lot. What that means is that almost all the people now living in apartments and a large number of those living in townhouses and high-rise condominium buildings are potential buyers for his single-family dwelling.

Furthermore, he points out, there is a great deal that an owner can do with a single-family home to increase its value. He plans to use his skills as a carpenter to finish the basement, build a wet bar in the family room, and maybe even add a room on the back. His wife is a talented gardener, and she intends to make their yard so beautiful that it will inspire envy — and action — throughout the neighborhood.

"What can you do to a condominium to increase its value while you live there?" Morris asks. "Maybe add some built-ins or put better tile in the bathroom. But when you sell it, some of your prospects might not want built-ins there or they might not care for the color of your tile."

Morris is as correct in his investment analysis as Virginia Moore, the condominium buyer, is in hers. For Morris, the ideal investment is a single-family home. He will make more profit because he will put more into it. Virginia Moore will pay less per square foot and sell in an increasingly stronger market for condominiums.

The point here is that one important fact in the choice of a home depends on the lifestyle of the investor. Condominiums are not for everyone; on the other hand, neither are single-family homes. Both can be good investments. Strictly from the standpoint of appreciation, however, the single-family home is generally the better purchase.

> The single-family home usually provides a better return on invested capital.

The Problems With Condominiums

CONDOMINIUMS have some drawbacks that a potential buyer must consider. The market is more limited. Families with school-age children usually want a home with a yard, which is fine with condominium residents who usually prefer not being in close quarters with a lot of children. But that is a large population group to cut off as potential buyers when the condominium owner wants to sell.

Another liability is that although the United States has survived more than 200 years of democracy, nobody is sure yet whether home investors can live happily in a majority-rule situation. Condominium buyers subject themselves to a homeowners association, one that can make decisions which some owners may not like but must live with. A buyer can, for example, find him or herself in a building where the majority of owners want to add all kinds of frills that will not only drive up homeowner association dues but also risk making the individual units so expensive as to be less desirable. Or the reverse could occur — the majority might

Condominium living isn't always easy, and it may or may not be profitable.

want to hold down costs to such an extent that needed maintenance is deferred, landscaping around the building is not improved, grass is not mowed often enough nor snow removed quickly enough, etc.; all of these factors would reduce the desirability of individual units.

Another consideration is that homeowners association dues are neither tax deductible nor predictable. In a single-family home, the owner maintains his or her own land and the exterior of the house. That is generally not a burdensome expense because rarely are high labor costs involved on a constant basis. Exterior maintenance of a condominium, however, is performed by people who are hired to do those jobs. On top of the basic costs of materials that both owners of single-family homes and condominiums pay for maintenance, the costs of labor and management and service personnel who run the building add to the expenses of the condominium resident.

Determining how much higher is a tricky business, too. The association dues increase according to inflationary trends, but they may also include major hikes if costs involving various common areas in the building should rise for one reason or another, or if major additions to the building's amenities — a swimming pool or more laundry equipment, for example — are desired by a majority of the residents. Then, special assessments are levied, and all the condominium owners must pay for the improvements or additions.

The rental apartment building that is converted to condominiums can offer certain advantages. The price per unit is often better because the buildings were constructed when costs were much lower than those involved in putting up new condominium structures. Additional advantages to buying into a converted building include the often desirable location, the larger living space and construction quality that many older apartment buildings possess, and the history of how much it has cost to run the building. Having such a history gives the buyer a realistic guide to the probable monthly assessment level.

On the other hand, some converted apartment buildings may have smaller rooms — especially bedrooms — than new condominiums, and tiny bedrooms can be a major drawback at resale time. An older building may also be suffering from a roof or an electrical system or a plumbing system that is in poor condition and in need of repair. Buildings put up for renters, moreover, may be lacking in many of the amenities that homeowners demand. For example, new condominium developers know how important soundproofing the walls can be to sales, and they spend extra money for quality there.

Buyers to whom a condominium investment seems to be the right way to go should first get some expert advice on how realistic the operating budget for the building seems to be. One way is to have the property manager of a similar condominium or apartment building go over (for a small fee, of course) the figures for the building in question. Another way is to consult an appraiser who can compare the cost figures of one building with those of other properties. Most of the people who have had bad experiences with condominiums have suffered because the original assessments were vastly underestimated. In fact, cases where these costs actually doubled a few months after a purchase are not uncommon.

Some Other Types Of Home Investment

SEVERAL VARIATIONS on the condominium concept offer advantages to the home investor. One is the townhouse condominium in which the owner does own some land — the property behind and in front of the home. Like the condominium resident, the townhouse owner also pays a monthly fee for maintenance of the areas between his property and other units and for any other facilities and services (snow removal, for example) that the residents share.

The advantage to this particular plan is that the owner can save money on exterior and yard maintenance by doing such work personally. Therefore, the dues paid to the homeowners association are generally less. The owner can also make some improvements to the property that will make the townhouse more valuable.

Another variation on the apartment-ownership principle is the cooperative, which is not really similar to a condominium except that owners occupy one unit and share common expenses with owners of other units in the building. Because the co-op, as it is often called, is so different from other types of residential investment property and is largely limited to a few major cities, it will not be covered at length in this book.

Briefly, however, a cooperative owner buys a share in a corporation or a percentage interest in a trust that owns the property and leases the individual unit which the buyer occupies. The main reason these units are not appealing to a home investor is that lenders will not supply a mortgage because there is no actual property put up as security. The cooperative buyer must come up with cash (or a loan other than a home mortgage) for the entire amount of the transaction.

Building Vs. Buying Standing Property

FOR THE INVESTOR seeking maximum profit, the single-family home on an individual lot appears to be the best way to go. But that brings up a variety of other questions. What kind of a house? On what lot? And where?

Maybe it will be a house you contract to build yourself on your own lot. A great many people who originally didn't know the first thing about building a house have already proved that it can be done. Peter and Jeanne Richardson, for example, built a house in a Chicago suburb that was worth 50 percent more on the day they finished it than they had spent to build it. Another couple who acted as contractor for the construction of their home in a Washington, D. C., suburb claimed a 10 to 12 percent saving over what a custom builder would have charged to build the home for them.

The Richardsons bought a lot in a subdivision that was being developed for custom building. Initially, they wanted to employ a custom builder to construct a particular home they had seen in a nearby development. But the cost of that home had risen beyond their range. Then they began exploring the idea of acting as their own contractors.

"When we started talking to subcontractors, we found them to be very helpful," Mrs. Richardson said. "We kept asking questions and found that they liked being teachers. We finally asked so many questions that we felt we knew what to do."

Unlike many tract builders, the Richardsons used quality materials, including such things as large stones for a fireplace. They did some of the work themselves, notably the bricklaying, and got additional help from family members.

Like the tract builders, however, the Richardsons took advantage of the sales tax deductions for income tax that builders normally take for the purchase of materials. For example, on the $14,000 worth of lumber used in the house, they were able to deduct the five percent sales tax — a $700 deduction on their income tax.

The Gerald Bachs had the same experience in building their Maryland home, especially the cooperation of helpful subcontractors. Starting with no knowledge at all of homebuilding, they emerged as authorities on such things as the short-term loans needed to cover construction costs before a mortgage on the completed property is obtained and on the various permits needed for water and sewer hookups, plumbing installation, and basic building.

The savings in building a home oneself may not be enough for many home investors, however. It is time-consuming to act as a contractor on a home, and dealing with the architect and the subcontractors can add up to more time than one can afford to give. It also stretches out the construction time, which can be considerable — at least eight months, according to one investor who has recently done it.

Final costs for a self-built home could be higher than anticipated because prices of materials may rise during the construction period. In addition, a custom-built house will always cost more than a tract home because the tract builder can buy in quantity — both land and materials. An individual may get some of the builder's discounts on materials, but probably not all of them because the builder is a steady customer.

Making changes during the progress of the construction can also add to the price of the self-built home. And although one gets exactly

Custom-building
a home
is risky,
but it can be
profitable
when done
prudently.

the house one desires (or close to it), a custom home may be so uniquely personal that its value may suffer at resale time.

Building or contracting for one's own home is certainly not for everybody. A custom-built home, however, with good features that appeal to a broad market and made of quality materials and construction is a valuable investment. Not only different, it is usually much better than what the conventional builder, preoccupied with low costs and quick sales, puts on the market.

Renovating Existing Homes

ANOTHER WAY TO go for people who want to invest themselves as well as their money in a home is to buy a structurally sound house for renovation or rehabilitation. This sort of an investment has been the source of profit for many people. And why not? A house that is run-down and is in need of work carries a bargain price for the space it offers. The upgrading process includes a number of improvements that almost anybody can do — e.g., painting, cleaning, sanding, etc. — which helps keep labor costs down.

Knowing someone with what renovaters call "talented hands" — the ability, that is, to handle all different aspects of construction — can mean even more profit to the home investor. These people are not as hard to find as one might think. The maintenance men in apartment buildings, for example, generally have skills to handle all kinds of problems that might occur, from wiring to mechanical systems to doors and windows that stick. In addition, they know carpentry, plumbing, furnaces, building codes, and almost everything else a rehabilitation investor needs. And many of these "talented hands" people are looking for extra work on their days off.

The advantage to renovating existing property is that the profit is almost immediate. A house that sells for $20,000 before a rehabilitation investment of $10,000 may very well carry a price tag of $40,000 six months after the work is completed — provided, of course, that the improvements are made properly.

The run-down home must be located in an area that is on the rise, however, or one where more expensive homes that are relatively well maintained are predominant. Putting money into renovation that will produce a house worth substantially more than the surrounding homes will not bring the return expected. The house will be too good for the neighborhood and will not command the resale price the renovation investor desires.

Investors in rehabilitation must get sound professional advice before buying because some homes cannot be rehabilitated without tremendous expense. An engineer or an architect can be very helpful here. The fee such a professional charges is usually about $200-$250, depending on whether the investor needs just a brief opinion or a full written report.

Illinois realtor Richard J. Hegner makes another important point: "The key to making a profit is 'restoration' and not remodeling. Unnecessary structural changes are costly and won't add to the value of the home. Do not modernize an older home so that the character of the dwelling is lost. Buyers interested in older homes want them to be clean, trouble-free, and convenient, but they don't want a 1977 interior in a 1910 shell."

Financing The Renovation

IN FINANCING a renovation, the investor's first stop after deciding on a property should be at the savings and loan association that is strongest in the area. The investor will likely get a most cordial reception. Lenders who have a heavy commitment in a neighborhood like nothing better than the fact that homes there are being renovated. It is good for business, protects their other loans there, and enables them to demonstrate their support for that neighborhood.

The investor's first meeting, however, is only preliminary — to get to know the lender, find out the current interest rate, and to be sure the lender handles rehabilitation loans. A more specific interview with the lender comes later when the investor has a plan describing exactly what is to be done and cost estimates as to what it will take to complete the renovation. Lenders will spend little time discussing dreams; they like facts such as bids and estimates from sub-contractors and an architect's plan if the investor plans to use an architect. When the potential buyer of a house for renovation has this type of information — including the names of contractors or subcontractors — that is the time to ask the lender for a loan to cover the cost of the house and its renovation.

That is the time, too, when the lender will begin to be more careful about the arrangements. Lenders are characteristically cautious, having seen enough schemes that for one reason or another have never been carried to fulfillment, leaving the lender holding title to a run-down house.

Therefore, the lender will insist on an appraisal at investor expense to be sure that the house will be worth as much after renovation as the amount of the loan plus 20 percent; the 20 percent represents the standard downpayment.

Next, the lender will evaluate the contractor and/or subcontractors to be sure that they produce good workmanship at a fair price. And finally, even when the loan is agreed to, many lenders will require that the investor's money go into the renovation before any of the lender's does. How does that work? Assume that one is asking for a $30,000 loan to cover the house and renovation costs. The lender might provide that amount if the appraisal shows that the property as renovated will be worth at least $36,000. But first, he wants the investor's money up front. He may ask the buyer to spend the first $6,000 in renovation costs before parting with the $30,000. That protects the lender by getting the borrower sufficiently invested with his own capital to insure the likelihood of the project being finished.

The Problems With Renovating

SEVERAL NEGATIVE points must be raised about rehabilitating homes for investment.

Getting in early in a neighborhood that is on the upgrade means living for some time with the people and the conditions that caused the neighborhood to decline; that can be an uncomfortable and sometimes even a dangerous experience.

If the home is going to be the investor's principal residence during the renovation, he or she will have to endure messy conditions and inconvenience for several months.

The overall cost of renovation may be higher than anticipated because the property requires more work than at first seemed likely.

Lenders may not provide the full 80 percent of after-renovation value because of the risk involved. Some financial institutions will loan only 70 percent of the value for a renovation project; in such instances, of course, the investor must come up with more initial capital.

If an area never really reverses its decline, the investor will end up owning just another house in an undesirable neighborhood. On the other hand, if the rehabilitation trend hits high gear before the investor is ready to buy, prices for unrenovated homes can rise so high that all one's work will not return the big profit expected.

Buying Existing Property

FOR MOST HOME investors, neither building or contracting for their own home nor rehabilitating an old house is practical, and owning a condominium may not be desirable. These investors just want to buy a good single-family house in an area that is going to appreciate faster than other areas, a home that they can improve and maintain so that it will someday provide a solid profit.

These people must ask themselves two basic questions: What can I afford and where should I buy?

What Should You Buy?

TO BENEFIT most from a home (or any other investment for that matter), the smart investor puts as little of his or her own money into the property as possible and buys the most expensive piece of property he or she can handle with that amount of money. A person who can buy a $35,000 house with nothing down — as veterans using the Veterans Administration loan guaranty program can often do — or someone who can buy a $100,000 house with a $5,000 downpayment stands to maximize the profit on a home investment.

Investment strategy in theory, however, is not necessarily wise and practical strategy for all home investors. Unless one has a good reserve, preferably in cash, the home buyer can run into big problems should anything happen to one's house, one's job, or oneself. The large monthly payments can be staggering in these circumstances because the investor is probably paying a high interest rate on top of a big mortgage, and it doesn't take a very heavy straw to break the back of a person struggling under such a large burden.

But the prudent home investor, while not taking on more of a burden than he or she can realistically expect to carry, is continually cognizant of investment strategy. For example, the difference in the percentage of profit on a home with a 20 percent downpayment and one with a 10 percent downpayment is 100 percent. In other words, the person who puts $5,000 down on a $50,000 home instead of the usual $10,000 and then sells the home a few years later for $60,000, makes a return on the $5,000 investment equivalent to 200 percent. A $10,000 downpayment on the same house would reduce the profit to 100 percent of the original investment.

The investor must calculate carefully how much debt he or she can incur safely. Someone who has 15 to 20 percent of a year's income in savings and also has some insurance, however, should seek out the maximum mortgage that he or she can afford in terms of monthly payments and that a lender will agree to provide.

Lenders can be a problem. They generally do

Extending oneself on a home
purchase can be dangerous
but wise investors buy
as much house as they can
possibly afford.

not like to make loans that result in monthly payments more than one week of an individual's pay. They also frown on loans that are higher than two and a half times a borrower's annual income. A person who earns $300 a week ($15,600 a year) will usually not find lenders sympathetic to mortgage payments of more than $300 a month on a home priced at more than $39,000.

Regional and state lending practices do differ, though. Some savings and loan associations in Hawaii, for example, allow borrowers to make monthly payments of up to 50 percent of monthly income, believing that the borrower will live frugally until he or she reaches higher income levels at which time the payments will not be so great a percentage of income. "And we've never had a foreclosure," says a savings and loan president who has participated in these loans.

Most people, however, should not burden themselves to that extent. They should buy within current means and figure on trading up to more valuable property later as their income increases.

A home investor who is confident that rising income will cover the monthly payments and will eventually alleviate the mortgage burden

---

The amount
to invest
in a downpayment
should be
directly proportional
to the anticipated
length of ownership.

---

may be able to find a lender who will agree to a 90 percent loan, the extra 10 percent guaranteed perhaps by a private mortgage company. Many of these companies are aggressively seeking business by trying to accommodate the needs of people whose income has been showing regular increases.

Investors who are eligible for FHA and GI loans can frequently find lenders who do not mind making high-ratio mortgages because such loans are guaranteed by the government. The downpayment required on a government-backed loan may be no more than five to 15 percent, and some VA loans involve no downpayment whatsoever.

A second mortgage — expensive because of the high interest rate it carries — may be worthwhile for some people who would not be able to buy a home otherwise. It may well carry a rate three percent above the conventional mortgage percentage, but in most instances the value of the property purchased will appreciate at an even greater rate, making the second mortgage attractive to people who could not enter the housing market without it.

When considering the amount of downpayment to put down, the investor should decide whether he or she is looking at a short-term or a long-term ownership period. A person buying for fast turnover should make the smallest downpayment consistent with the monthly payments he or she can afford on the most expensive property a lender is willing to finance. If things work out and the property grows in value by 20 percent in three to five years, the investor will realize a handsome profit. A person who expects to be in the home for 10 years or longer, however, should put down a larger amount and use the money that is not going out in big monthly mortgage payments to improve the house.

Remember, however, that mortgage payments are not the only expense of homeownership. Just furnishing a house can cost thousands of dollars, and estimates of the costs for heating and cooling, utilities, repairs, maintenance, and materials can range from 10 percent to more than 15 percent of the cost of the home.

Where You Should Buy

AFTER THE investor establishes how much he or she can afford, it is time to make another very important decision — where to buy. The right choice of location when purchasing a home almost guarantees a profit.

It is vital to the value appreciation of property that healthy influences be observable, espe-cially in older neighborhoods. Anything that makes the neighborhood more convenient can add to property value. For example, extension of the transit system, development of a com-munity shopping center nearby, establishment of a medical center or community college would all add to the convenience and value of homes

in the area.

To the family with young children, possibly no single factor is as important as the quality of the school district. To be within walking distance of a good school is one of the finest geographic advantages a home can have, perhaps exceeded only by the proximity to good transportation. Many existing homes have both of these advantages, and their owners generally experience little difficulty in reaping substantial profits at resale time.

The existing home in a good neighborhood generally offers established landscaping, a functioning school district, and reasonably stable taxes because schools and community improvements are completed or are well on their way to being so. But is the best location at present also the best place to buy for future profit? Surprisingly, the answer is no.

Ed Hoffman, vice president of the national building company Hoffman Homes, sums up one of the basic considerations. "There is an axiom in real estate that if distance is no problem, the farther you are willing to go from an urban center, the more house you can expect from your investment. This is still valid because in the relatively younger and newer communities, more of the money is going into the house than into the community, which is still maturing. The same dollar spent in a mature community pays for good location instead of just the house."

The best-located property is usually the most expensive. Since it has been recognized as prime real estate for a long time, it has already experienced its best days of value appreciation — at least in terms of percentage increases.

Consider, for example, two homes of the same size in two such different locations that one is worth $90,000 and the other home is worth $40,000. Perhaps enough people want to live in the prime area to push the price to $100,000 in a year — a good 11 percent gain. But the $40,000 home in a rapidly growing area stands a better chance of going up 11 percent and of showing that kind of gain for several years.

In addition, the owner of the $40,000 house

has invested perhaps $8,000, while the owner of the $90,000 property has probably paid a minimum of $18,000 down. The lower the downpayment, remember, the better the return. In prime real estate areas, moreover, maintenance costs are usually higher, taxes are higher, and the resale market is getting thinner because fewer people each year can afford the expensive price tags on the homes there.

Thus the investor who is attempting to turn over a home for maximum profit should avoid the stable, established neighborhoods. This investor should be looking at well-built homes in the new areas where values someday will be as high as those commanded by property in the best areas of town.

Beware Of The Boom Towns

BOOM AREAS must be watched closely, however. There is a suburb southeast of Chicago that in the early 1970's showed all the signs of a boom. When an interstate highway opened nearby, developers flocked in to build housing, shopping centers, and a few industrial strips. But by 1976, it was difficult to sell a home in this area at even a respectable profit. The reasons exist in the sudden, massive amount of housing (all in approximately the same price range) erected there and the absence of planning that went into the community's preparation for growth.

Specifically, the area lacked sufficient industry to support all those new $35,000-$45,000 homes. The result was a glut of new housing that forced anybody trying to resell a home into facing a buyer's market. Naturally, homes in this suburb did not provide the kind of investment return that their owners had expected at the time of purchase.

Perhaps 10 years from now, that community will offer good prospects for profitable investment. The village government has since made it expensive — if not impossible — for developers to build any substantial amount of additional housing there by placing restrictions on land use. Homeowners living in the community now, however, face an uncertain future regarding the fate of their home investment. When a community booms so fast that the local government cannot provide schools and services and when builders construct an enormous number of homes in the same price range, the smart home buyer approaches the situation very carefully, often waiting to see whether the community in question will turn out to be an authentic boom area before investing there.

Some of the best real estate profits in recent years have come from investments in attractive residential communities near major new regional shopping centers. These centers offer several advantages to nearby residents; not only do they make shopping convenient, but they also contribute so much to the local tax base that property taxes are usually lower than in other communities. They also inspire other development in the community, especially office buildings that bring in new jobs and new residents. The negative aspects of a regional shopping center affect housing that is very close to the center, particularly the immediate neighborhoods that suffer from the traffic volume going to and from the stores. Fortunately, these negative aspects are generally easy for the home investor to perceive and avoid.

Another influence on making residential property profitable has been the office park. Filled with white collar workers who want to live near their offices, these developments have contributed greatly to nearby residential property values. They also contribute to the tax base, cause few problems (except traffic), and inspire other businesses to locate in the community.

Potential buyers looking at new housing in new areas should keep these criteria in mind:

- Proximity to shopping centers or office parks.
- Development of a master plan by the community so that growth continues but along well-conceived lines.
- Variety in housing so that not all of it is aimed at the same segment of the market.
- Absence of heavy traffic from the shopping center of offices in the area or intended purchase.

Style And Value

FINALLY, a word should be said about housing style. It has been proven to the satisfaction of almost every builder that some styles do not belong in certain geographic areas. In the Midwest, for example, the California look — with its soaring lines and abundance of glass and wood — will find a very small market among people who like their homes to look strong and sturdy. By the same token, the solid midwestern brick or stately southern colonial will appeal to few Californians. A house that is noticeably out of place suffers at resale time, and the intelligent home investor buys the type of property consistent with market preferences.

Follow The Experts

ONE OF THE surest ways to find growth areas is to take advantage of the marketing expertise of banks, franchise operators, and grocery chains. Before they invest in an area, they research the market extensively for signs of stable growth. They evaluate past trends in the area, and they use this knowledge to make intelligent estimates of future developments. These commercial investors make a science out of anticipating area growth trends, and they are willing to risk their dollars to back up their growth projections. Since their judgments are usually right, the smart home investor looks to the experts before purchasing property for profit.

What and where to buy are two of the most important decisions that the home investor makes. In the end, a wise purchase almost always returns a substantial profit, while the wrong purchase can prove a very costly mistake even at a time when nearly all residential real estate values are escalating. Successful home investment is not difficult, however, for individuals who approach the situation carefully and who understand how potentially profitable property can be acquired.

Of Buying

THE KEY DETERMINATION one must make when shopping for a home is deciding whether one is dealing with a buyer's market or a seller's market. The entire strategy of selecting, bargaining, and closing at the best price depends on the relative strength of the buyer as opposed to the seller in a particular market at a particular time.

A buyer's market is characterized by the following factors:

- More homes are available for sale than there are people qualified or desirous of buying them.

- Some homes in the area have already sold at prices well below those at which they were originally listed.

- Owners show a willingness to make concessions in the financing of the property — e.g., offering a second mortgage so that the buyer need not come up with a big downpayment.

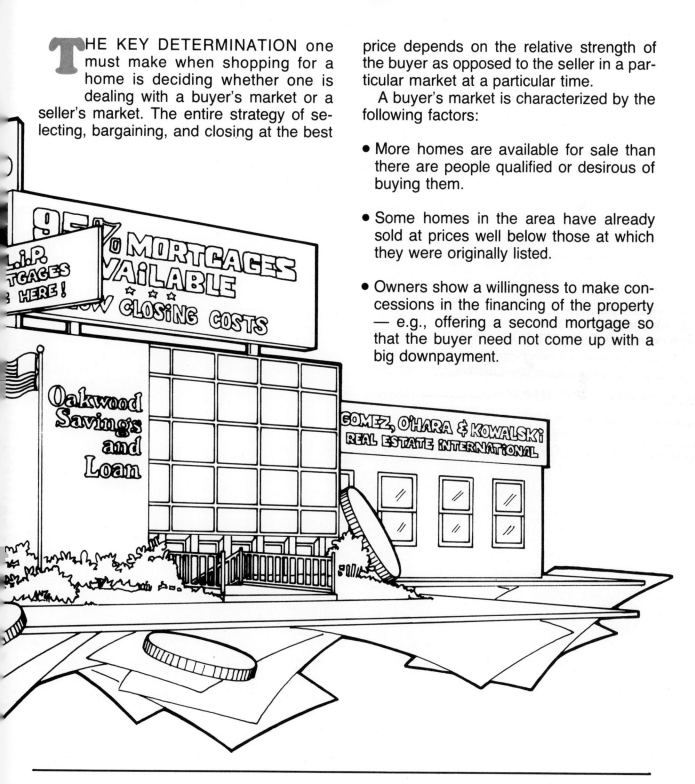

These same characteristics could also apply to a neighborhood in decline, however. Therefore, further distinctions must be made. The buyer's market is one that is broad in scope and not confined to a single locality or neighborhood. The downward trend in property values is transitory, not continual. Usually, buyer's markets coincide with tight mortgage money conditions, at which time buyers who can get credit can drive a hard bargain.

More frequently, though, a buyer encounters a seller's market, especially in the neighborhoods where owners have been enjoying maximum home investment profits. The seller knows how much comparable properties in the area have sold for and will accept no less. The buyer who intends to get a good deal in a seller's market had better be a shrewd negotiator or have access to a competent broker.

The broker knows the prices of listed properties sold recently in the immediate area and can spot trends up or down in specific neighborhoods. What the buyer wants is a broker who will try to understand particular needs and desires regarding the home to be purchased and who will be helpful in the negotiations by suggesting various compromises that will result in a satisfactory transaction.

The good broker shows the buyer properties that best suit particular purposes. Many real estate salespeople insist on showing every home that fits a prospect's budget, but the smart home investor doesn't want to see many of those houses. The property must have certain characteristics to be a good investment, and all too frequently the buyer must repeat these characteristics to the broker time and again in order to make them understood.

Before getting involved with a broker or an agent, the buyer should request an interview. Among the important points to learn in an interview are whether the real estate agent thinks of homes as investments and whether he or she has made any personal real estate investments recently. After sizing up the person's responses to this approach, the prospective buyer can make a reasonable assessment as to whether the agent will provide the necessary services and advice or whether the search for an investment-oriented broker should continue.

If the buyer has narrowed the search for a new home to a few neighborhoods, then it is good strategy in most cases to talk to the broker or brokers who seem to have the dominant position there. An agency that handles most of the sales in an area generally knows the individual owners and the homes. That's the agency with whom the buyer should work.

Not all homes are sold through brokers, however, and the wise home investor is ever watchful for homes put up for sale by their owners. Quite often, these are the best homes; the owner who tries to sell his or her own property is usually marketing an excellent home that he or she anticipates no difficulty in selling. To assure that it moves quickly, though, the owner prices the home at an attractive level, figuring to make a good profit anyway because there is no broker involved to take a commission.

The process of buying sounds simple: just narrow the choices down to the type of home that fits one's lifestyle and then select the one that offers the best profit potential. In reality, the process is a good deal more complicated, involving a host of specific criteria as well as knowledge of negotiating, financing, and closing on the home to best advantage.

Selecting The Residence

JAN AND HARRY Cleland did almost everything right when they moved to Washington, D.C., in 1972 to work for a newly elected United States senator. First, they settled into an apartment with a one-year lease in order to study and become familiar with the metropolitan area before committing themselves to buy a home. Then, they did some serious research and analysis.

They soon spotted two areas that seemed to have the dynamic character which would enable current home values to increase rapidly. These areas were expanding, and builders were already concentrating there. These areas also contained solid communities with an established school system, and the population growth was being absorbed without great controversy or additional taxation.

Moreover, local authorities in these areas had already approved land for the development of major new shopping centers, and the federal government was building interstate highway hookups through both areas — including a beltway around the District of Columbia that cut a half hour or more each way off the traveling time to the popular Maryland and Delaware beaches and to the Chesapeake Bay marinas.

The beltway and the new shopping centers made property in Fairfax County, Virginia, and western Montgomery County, Maryland, more desirable — and therefore more valuable — almost overnight. Less populated than Arlington County due south of Washington, where the volume of commuters choked the principal highway into the nation's capital, Fairfax and Montgomery were also less expensive to live in than the most desirable parts of the city itself. The Clelands knew that they could not afford the expensive city homes, and they began thinking seriously about buying a home in one of the attractive outlying areas.

After reading about the areas in the papers, the Clelands began asking people. Then they went out to evaluate the areas first-hand. Taking a map with them, the Clelands marked in where the new highways and regional shopping centers would be. They wanted to be close to these facilities but not too close. Finally, they set out to look at the individual neighborhoods.

Eventually, the Clelands narrowed their choices down to two neighborhoods in Fairfax County. They called the two brokers who dominated sales in those neighborhoods, found satisfactory agents to work with in each company, and asked to be notified when any property was put up for sale that seemed appropriate to their plans. Each time the Clelands looked at a property with the sales agent they also made their own survey of the neighborhood, checking to see if anything had been put on the market by the owner or offered so recently that their broker didn't know about it yet.

The Clelands were right about the growth prospects for Fairfax County, especially the areas near the new Tyson's Corner shopping mall and the Capital Beltway. They were also right about the neighborhoods, which offered the stability and well-maintained appearance that prove so highly attractive at resale time. And they were right about the house they eventually chose after looking at perhaps 15 homes in their carefully selected Fairfax County neighborhoods.

Smart investors
survey areas
and neighborhoods,
seeking homes
having potential
for profit.

Choosing The Home With Profit Potential

GENERALLY SPEAKING, the home buyer can find several properties that will provide a satisfactory level of comfort and convenience. To earn the highest return on one's housing dollars, however, it pays to wait until the right property in terms of profit potential comes along. Such a house can be identified in several ways.

It should have eye appeal. Something about it will set it off a bit from the rest of the homes in the neighborhood. Usually, it will have more or fuller trees, a neater lawn and more flowers, and look fresh and well maintained.

A house that has great eye appeal usually sells for a price that reflects that appeal. There are houses, though, that have the potential to stand out in the neighborhood (a potential unrealized by their current owners), which sell for bargain prices by comparison with surrounding homes. Turning a house that *could* be into one that *is* eye appealing can produce thousands of dollars in value appreciation for the new owner.

In fact, that is always something to think about when evaluating a home — what could be done to make it something special? Could those tiny bedrooms that so detract from the home's desirability be combined into a spacious master bedroom suite with a small sitting area or dressing room and a single large bedroom? Would the enclosing of an unattractive screened porch provide more needed living area or answer the need for a den or children's playroom? What would it cost to update the kitchen and/or enlarge it to provide more work space or a breakfast eating area?

Before going shopping, it would be advisable for the prospective home investor to talk to a contractor or some other knowledgeable person who can give good advice about the costs of improvements. It is better to find out how feasible home improvement plans are before buying the house. Some bedrooms can't be combined, some screened porches can't be enclosed, and some kitchen remodeling can't be completed without extensive rewiring and plumbing work. The smart buyer always knows

> The "right" property has — or could have — eye appeal.

how much the transformation will cost before making any commitments.

As important as eye appeal is the condition of the house. All systems should work well in a home for which the seller is asking top dollar.

Generally speaking, a home constructed by a builder who enjoys a reputation for using quality materials and skilled tradesmen can be counted on for at least 15 years without major breakdowns. The roof may need replacement within that period if weather conditions are harsh, and some rewiring may be needed to accommodate more and heavier appliances or a new central air conditioning system. Of course, a heating system that works hard for six months or more out of the year may need a couple of overhauls within the first 15 years.

But 15 years is typically the smooth sailing period for a new home. In fact, many builders today offer a 10-year warranty which — for a small annual charge — protects the buyer against breakdowns in the home's major systems. Called the Home Owners Warranty Plan, it can be a worthwhile investment even though nothing really should go wrong for that period and five years beyond.

Builders establish their reputations by staying in business in the same community for many years. Some build just a few homes a year, but they build these homes sturdily on well-located lots in developing neighborhoods. Frequently, they build these homes on speculation, assuming that the inherent quality and attractiveness of the residences will attract buyers.

The Process Of Buying

Getting An Appraisal And Other Professional Advice

THE LENDER WHO is going to finance the home can help the prospective buyer in other ways as well. He generally knows the reputations of the major builders in the area, and he can supply an appraiser to evaluate what the property is worth. The appraisal costs the buyer some money, typically $75 to $150, but it is generally money well spent. A professional appraisal can be very useful in both buying the home and again later when selling it.

On residential property, an appraiser who works for a mortgage lending institution will inspect the property after an application for a loan has been received. The appraiser estimates the value of the property because the lender needs to know how much he could get for the property were the borrower to fail to make payments and the mortgage go into default.

The appraiser's report is usually made on a two- to four-page form. Frequently, lenders will supply a copy of the report to the buyer, but sometimes they will only reveal the figure on the bottom line — the appraiser's estimate of the market value for the house and lot.

The buyer who wants a full appraisal report but whose lender will not provide one can hire an independent appraiser listed in the classified section of the telephone directory under "Appraisers — Real Estate." Some of the appraisers listed do not handle house appraisals, specializing instead in larger properties or property involving machinery and equipment as well as real estate. These appraisers' names are followed by the designations MAI (Member of the Appraisal Institute), SREA (Senior Real Estate Analyst of the Society of Real Estate Appraisers), or ASA (American Society of Appraisers). The residential specialists usually have RM (Residential Member of the Appraisal Institute) or SRA (Senior Residential Appraiser of the Society of Real Estate Appraisers) after their names, or else they indicate in their listings that they will appraise residential property.

Appraisers frequently fail to give clients all the information the buyers should have about the physical condition of houses. The appraisal process has become largely one of comparing properties that have been sold recently with the property being appraised. Most appraisers believe that the only accurate way to estimate value is to know what a willing buyer would pay a willing seller for the property after it has been on the market long enough to attract interest. Therefore, the appraisal report will contain information about the sales of property like the one appraised, a few comments about the condition of the property, and a summary of the appraiser's reasoning in arriving at the final estimate of value.

To get more out of an appraiser, the buyer should make clear in the beginning that a thorough inspection of the heating and plumbing systems and the adequacy of the wiring is expected. Some appraisers will admit that they are not qualified to evaluate these systems and suggest another appraiser who is. Others are able to make such evaluations, but they don't do so as a practice because they think such information has little to do with a home's market value in the eyes of most buyers.

There are several other sources for information about the condition of a home for sale besides what an appraiser supplies. In most major metropolitan areas, home inspection specialists are available at a reasonable fee ($75 to $150 in most cases) who can evaluate the condition of a house. The specialists provide reports that can be useful in avoiding the purchase of a home needing expensive repairs, and it can also serve as an effective negotiating tool. By showing the seller an objective report from an expert who says that the heating system is inefficient and will require a sizable expenditure to put it in top working order, the buyer may be able to persuade the seller to reduce the price of the home somewhat.

In most cities, the utility companies also will help buyers evaluate the adequacy of the heating and cooling systems. Their representatives will inspect the systems and provide useful information on what could be and what should be done. Since installing a central air conditioning system represents one of the best home improvements in terms of return on investment at resale, the information that the utility company provides in this regard can be extremely important to the home investor seeking maximum profitability.

Any layman without the knowledge to judge the adequacy and condition of the functional components of a house should have one or more of these experts inspect the property before investing in it. Getting an expert's opinion is especially important when the home under consideration is more than 15 years old.

Inspecting The Home

SOME HOMES ARE simply examples of shoddy construction; they are built with cheap materials, and they lack adequate facilities for hot water, electricity, and heat. A good sign that a house under consideration does not fall into this category is evidence that it was originally built or financed by the Federal Housing Administration or Veterans Administration. Homes that were granted mortgages insured by these agencies had to meet the FHA's Minimum Property Standards, good assurance that the materials and craftsmanship that went into the home were not cheap or shoddy.

Signs of shoddy construction or poor home maintenance can be visible even to the inexperienced eyes of the prospective buyer. The wise home investor — even the novice — can inspect a home carefully for telltale signs of present or future problems, noting especially . . .

- Any areas where water appears to be coming in where it is not supposed to or seems to have infiltrated at some earlier date. An unevenly painted ceiling or wall, a mildew odor in the basement, evidence of replastering or retiling in just one area of a room might all be signs that water leakage has occurred.

- A lack of water pressure. By flushing toilets and turning on both hot and cold water faucets at the same time the buyer can quickly see whether water pressure is ade-

quate. Manipulating both faucets together and letting them run for a few seconds makes it easy to find out whether the temperature can be adjusted accurately and whether once adjusted it remains constant.

- The condition of the septic system in homes that have private waste disposal facilities. After asking when the septic system was last inspected and cleaned, the prospective buyer should stand near the tank and see if any odor is coming from it or if there are any soggy areas around it. A septic system that is cleaned every two or three years should last for about 30 years, but it eventually will have to be replaced. A small home should have a tank of at least 750 gallons capacity, while a three-bedroom house should have a tank capacity of 900 gallons. Add 250 gallons of capacity per bedroom for homes larger than three bedrooms.

- The date and results of the last termite inspection. If no inspection has been made in the last two years, the buyer should arrange for an immediate inspection (especially important for a frame home) or make provision in any contract to buy that the sale is subject to a satisfactory termite inspection.

- The efficiency of the heating system. The prospective purchaser should request that the thermostat setting be altered — raised if it's cold outside and lowered if it's warm — and then see how fast the room heats up or cools down. It should take no more than half an hour for the home to reach the desired temperature.

Even a novice can spot problems.

● Last year's heating and cooling bills. Usually, the costs of heating and cooling are included on information that a real estate broker puts into the listing card, but the buyer should not be reluctant to ask an owner for utility bills or for cancelled checks to the utility companies. The utilities themselves will provide information regarding typical costs for heating or cooling a home of a specific size. If the bills for the home in question are much higher, then the prospective buyer can justifiably conclude that the structure requires better insulation.

● The main electrical cable coming into the house. If the cable is about an inch thick, the home probably has 100 amp service, which is the minimum wiring standard and adequate to operate lighting, small appliances, and a good deal of major electrical equipment. At least 200 amp service is needed for a home that is electrically heated and cooled, however. Minimum standards found in building codes provide for both 120 and 240 volt circuits (the latter for major equipment) and a capacity of 24,000 watts — although a capacity of 36,000 or more watts is needed for electric heating and cooling.

Those are the main items that any layman can size up about a house. If this limited inspection turns up problem areas, then it would be worth the expense to hire an expert to take a look. To profit from a home, it behooves the owner to minimize operational costs as much as possible, and that can only be done when the structure purchased is in reasonably good condition.

Assessing A Home's Livability

BEYOND THE HOME'S structural or mechanical defects, the buyer must assess how livable the residence will be; that means evaluating the floor plan. There's very little one can do about a home with an unlivable floor plan after purchasing it — at least, not without considerable expense.

Here are some floor plan problems as outlined by John L. Domeier, chairman of Great American Federal Savings and Loan Association in Chicago.

● A home should have three basic zones, all buffered from each other by halls or closets or bathrooms. One area should provide space

The Extras Buyers Are Seeking

BUILDERS HAVE LEARNED — through both market research and their own experience — that homes sell faster and at greater profit if they include the extras that particular types of buyers find appealing. The following checklist can be helpful to home investors because it breaks down the extras into groups appropriate to buyers of various ages and lifestyles.

The Family With School-Age Children. Profile: parents in their 20's to mid-40's; one to three children; first- or second-time buyers; income rising.

Item	Already Provided	Could Be Added
Large family room or playroom	_____	_____
High quality schools (public, private, and parochial)	_____	_____
Nearby recreational facilities	_____	_____
Finished basement or attic	_____	_____
Large lot, especially a large back yard	_____	_____
Kitchen with dining area that seats the whole family	_____	_____

Item	Already Provided	Could Be Added
Good visibility from kitchen to family room, allowing parent to check on small children	_____	_____
Bedroom/bathroom area for parents well separated from children's rooms	_____	_____
Extra storage space in garage for bicycles and yard maintenance equipment	_____	_____
A "mud room" entry where children can clean shoes and store toys before entering the main part of the house	_____	_____

The Working Family. *Profile: both members of couple working; no immediate plans for children; former apartment dwellers seeking space and tax advantages; first-time buyers.*

Lot is easily maintained or cared for by an owners association	_____	_____
Shopping is close enough for walking or a short car trip	_____	_____
Movies, libraries and/or book stores, and recreational facilities are nearby	_____	_____
Washer and dryer are included	_____	_____
Fireplace is included	_____	_____
Kitchen has a small dining area	_____	_____

The Empty Nester. *Profile: couple with children away at school or married and living elsewhere; have owned at least one home previously; last home too large for current needs; tired of maintaining big home and lot; own plenty of large pieces of furniture; possess lifetime collections or memorabilia to display and store.*

Lot easy to maintain or maintained by owners' association	_____	_____
Several open walls for positioning large pieces of furniture	_____	_____
Master bedroom suite (large bedroom, sitting room or dressing room, walk-in or extremely large closet, separate bath)	_____	_____
Second bedroom that could be combination den/guest room	_____	_____
Separate dining room	_____	_____
Two-car heated garage	_____	_____
Self-cleaning appliances	_____	_____
Large kitchen with extra counter and cabinet space	_____	_____
Good security system	_____	_____
Well insulated	_____	_____
Extra storage space	_____	_____

Two other major groups should be mentioned because they represent significant segments of the total home-buyer market: singles and retirees. Singles look for somewhat the same amenities and extras as the working family, while retirees generally are seeking the same items as the empty nester.

for food preparation, washing clothes, and active hobbies. Another should provide privacy and quiet in a separate area — i.e., where the bedrooms are located. Shared activity occurs in yet another zone — the living room, eating areas, and family room.

Zoning is most easily achieved in a two-story or split-level house, where the bedrooms are upstairs and all the other areas are downstairs. In a ranch or one-story design, the bedrooms may be in one wing, living room and dining room in the middle, and kitchen and utility room in the opposite wing. The best floor plans have these three zones properly separated.

- Inefficient traffic flow can cause furnishing problems and a great deal of inconvenience. Traffic flow refers to the way people get from one part of the house to another. The best traffic flow is one where people do not have to walk through one room to get to another. For example, it is advantageous to be able to reach the kitchen directly from the garage, permitting members of the family to bring in groceries or take out garbage without walking through the living areas. Being able to reach the family room from the bedrooms without walking through the kitchen or living room is also desirable, as is getting to the bathrooms without passing through a bedroom or other rooms en route.

- Adequate storage space is particularly important if the home is small. Buyers moving from big homes to condominiums or townhouses, for example, face the problem of storing a lifetime of possessions which they don't want to give up. Therefore, the home they seek must have storage room somewhere — in closets, cabinets, attic, crawl space, basement, or garage.

- Rooms should be big enough to accommodate large pieces of furniture. Many people own oversized pieces of furniture — from king-sized beds to antique breakfronts — and such people should look for plenty of open wall space, space that is free of heating vents and radiators.

When a person buys a home for investment, it is essential that he or she think about the potential buyers who would find the property appealing when it comes time to put the property back on the market again. Home builders develop what they call a profile of their most likely buyers before they even start construction of a house, and then include features that the potential buyers will appreciate. The home investor should think in the same terms, both in selecting the residence to buy and in improving the property during ownership.

For example, a home with only two bedrooms probably will not appeal to a family with children, even if the house is located in a good school district, as much as a home will that has three or four bedrooms. On the other hand, a two-bedroom home with plenty of wall space for large pieces of furniture, big rooms, and plenty of storage will probably find a good market among "empty nesters," couples whose children have left home to attend college or start their own households. A two-bedroom home without these amenities will likely appeal only to singles, and that means a limited market when trying to realize the highest profit at resale.

Buying The Very New Or The Very Old Home

MUCH CAN BE said for buying a brand new home instead of purchasing an existing residence. The new home generally has all the latest features and appliances, and it allows the buyer to make choices regarding the type and color of tile, carpeting, flooring, cabinetry, and wall coverings.

It usually is good investment strategy when buying a new home to upgrade the kitchen cabinets and bathroom fixtures, especially if the builder's standard components fail to give the appearance of good quality. A fireplace can be worth having if the home's primary appeal is to the working couple or to the family with school-age children. Expenditures on better grade carpeting and tile, on the other hand, seldom return their cost at resale because the carpet looks worn and the color of the tile is sure to displease some prospects.

A few builders allow the buyer to make

changes in the basic home pattern, including making rooms larger or leaving some rooms unfinished. The risk in customizing, though, lies in the possibility that the buyer will create a home that no one else would want. Thus, in addition to being expensive, custom designing can be counterproductive in terms of profit.

Buying what is called an unfinished house can make good sense from an investment standpoint. During the mid-1970's, when first-time home buyers were increasingly being priced out of the market, builders started offering homes that were unfinished in certain respects. A bathroom, for example, would have the roughed-in plumbing and the heating and cooling vents, but it was unfinished in terms of fixtures, decorating, etc. The idea was to sell the home for less money, allowing the buyer to save on labor costs either by finishing the area him or herself or letting the area remain unfinished until sufficient funds could be accumulated to hire skilled laborers. The idea of marketing an unfinished house caught on, and today it represents a good way for a buyer who would otherwise be excluded from the housing market to buy a first home.

It is much better to buy a new home in a subdivision that already looks attractive and somewhat settled than to move into an area where the builder has bulldozed all the trees to save construction costs. If the builder has not saved some of the trees or spent the money to bring in large young trees, the whole improvement of the subdivision will depend on the individual landscaping skills and budgets of the new homeowners. The prudent home investor tries to minimize his or her dependence on these unknown factors.

Frequently, the new home can be financed more advantageously than an existing residence. Builders often have a commitment from a lender to provide mortgage money at an interest rate slightly below the market level. They also are willing, in most cases, to finance their homes with low-interest, low-down-payment loans insured by the Federal Housing Administration or Veterans Administration.

In good markets, builders announce a price for their homes and that's it. There is much less

> There is money
> to be made in
> both new construction
> and old residences,
> with successful
> investors
> knowing what
> they are getting
> and how to maximize
> the return
> on their property.

negotiation involved in buying a new home than in buying an existing residence. Only on a few occasions have buyers been able to force builders to back off from listed prices, and those were times of extraordinary mortgage money shortages. Generally speaking, the earlier one can buy a new home the better. In addition to pre-opening sales — at which time homes are at their least expensive — the buyer profits through purchasing early because prices for materials and labor are sure to keep rising by at least the rate of inflation.

At the opposite extreme from the brand new house is the very old house. The best of these homes are usually located in areas where restoration is underway or where most homes have been well maintained right along and no signs of decline are detectable. In such cases, the profit potential is considerable, especially if the home investor finds a gem that just needs time and effort to restore to its original splendor.

The gems are few and far between, however, and investors must be wary of becoming so captivated with the architecture and the spaciousness and the special touches of an old home that they fail to check such practical aspects as what it costs to heat or cool the house. In fact, it is almost always essential for a buyer to hire a contractor, architect, or engineer to examine the old house and determine what needs to be done and how much it would cost to do it.

When buying an obviously flawed house, new or old, the investor should have an attorney establish in the contract of sale that the seller will cover the cost of putting the house in acceptable condition — i.e., repairing and replacing what needs to be repaired and replaced. If the seller refuses to accept these conditions, as sellers often will when they know that they can get rid of a home without making any concessions, the investor must decide whether the cost of the repairs or replacements is worth the risk of losing the home. It is such an individual decision that it is difficult to establish any general rules as to what to do in any given situation.

The point is, however, that no smart home investor buys in ignorance. The idea is to know what one is getting, how much it will cost to have any problems fixed, and then using this knowledge to negotiate from strength by pointing out shortcomings of the property to the seller.

The seller may decide to offer the buyer a reduction in the price of the home equal to the amount required to make the repairs. Another arrangement for the buyer is to agree in the sales contract that the seller will pay in cash an amount equal to the cost of the repairs or replacements. This arrangement gives the buyer an opportunity to improve the property at a time of his or her choosing, but it poses the problem of collecting money from a seller who may not even remain in the area. Either way, though — a price reduction or a cash payment — is better than having the seller simply promise to take care of the defects before the closing date.

The lender in the deal, however, might not agree to go forward with a loan on a home lacking, for example, a good heating plant. He might insist on pegging the market value of the house lower in order to compensate for the defects. If he sees that replacement of the heating system is provided for in the sales contract, he is certain to look upon the needed mortgage more favorably, and an offer to leave money in escrow for the necessary repairs generally convinces the most reluctant lender to go ahead with the loan.

Purchasers
of new homes
should upgrade
only those areas
that will return
the extra
expenditure
at resale.

Negotiating For The Home

The Process Of Buying

NEGOTIATION IS MERELY the means of discovering how much the seller is willing to concede to sell the home and how much the buyer is willing to pay to obtain a particular property. Some sellers — especially in a seller's market — will refuse to make any concessions because they know they don't have to. In such cases, the buyer must acquiesce to the seller's terms or else sacrifice purchase of the home. In many more instances, though, effective negotiation is clearly worthwhile, saving the buyer many thousands of dollars off the original price.

The broker is of little help to the home investor in reducing the seller's price. While real estate salespeople can be extremely useful in pushing promising negotiations to a conclusion, they should not be relied upon for guidance as to when to demand and when to give in on price. It would be an unusual real estate agent who would jeopardize his or her commission by urging a buyer to hold firm. The real estate agent or broker is hired by and paid by the seller, not the buyer, and the seller's interests are therefore protected first and foremost.

The investor's own analysis of the home for sale and of prices of comparable properties in the area should provide all the guidance needed for submitting an initial bid. The idea is to make an offer that neither insults the owner nor is so high as to diminish the potential for profit in the investment.

In addition to price, real estate negotiation involves timing (the seller's urgency to get out and the buyer's urgency to get in), determining what is real estate — and thus part of the property — and what is personal property, finding the kind of financing each party can accept, and deciding when to close the deal and sign the papers. In all of these respects, the broker can be extremely important. Not many buyers want to get involved in haggling with sellers, and the broker can help avoid a great deal of unpleasantness by dealing between the two parties.

The first thing the broker can do is submit the offer to buy. Submitted in writing, the offer may be below the seller's expectations, but it cannot be dismissed because it generally comes ac-

> Buyers cannot count on brokers or agents for help in reducing the seller's price.

companied by a deposit known as earnest money. Usually, this amount ($500 or more) is not refundable if the seller agrees to the contract and the buyer later backs out.

Many successful home investors make an initial offer 10 percent below what they consider to be the home's actual market value. It should be emphasized that this figure is not 10 percent below the seller's price; sellers frequently start at least 10 percent over what they expect to get, and often higher than that.

The offer to buy should include any conditions that the buyer wants the seller to meet before agreement can be reached. Repair or replacement of any defective equipment, for example, would be specifically listed as a condition of sale. So would any concessions in financing, such as the seller's agreement to accept a second mortgage in order to reduce the buyer's downpayment. The contract could also be made conditional on when the buyer is able to take possession or on when the buyer is able either to obtain a loan or sell a previous home.

These conditions should be reviewed by an attorney prior to submission of the offer to the seller. A broker is not qualified to practice law, and he or she does not have the buyer's interests at heart as the buyer's personal attorney should have. The broker, of course, wants every deal to go through as rapidly as possible.

An important section of the offer to buy is a physical description of the property, which should include all those items that are not part of the real estate but which the buyer wants for the price specified. Carpeting, draperies, room air conditioners, refrigerators, etc., must be listed in the description of what is being exchanged. Too often buyers find after closing that items they assumed were part of the purchase have been taken by the sellers. Unless those items were listed in the contract to buy, however, sellers were under no obligation to leave them behind.

If the initial offer to buy is rejected, the prospective buyer starts negotiating by making concessions until a satisfactory agreement is reached. In addition to raising the price, the buyer can offer other benefits to the seller that might secure an agreement. The following benefits frequently turn a rejected offer into an accepted one — even when no alteration of the purchase price is involved.

- Conventional financing instead of government-insured financing to save the seller the one-time charges that the lender generally demands when the loan is insured by FHA or VA.

- An offer to purchase some items that the owner wanted to sell but which the prospective buyer had previously excluded.

- Waiver of previously specified repairs that the owner was asked to make as a condition of sale.

- An offer either to speed up or delay the closing process in order to suit the convenience of the seller.

Sometimes the seller needs the additional cash that selling carpeting or lawn maintenance equipment will bring, and thus will agree to the buyer's terms with that one minor concession

thrown in. Flexibility on financing or timing can also gain the house on a buyer's terms. When successful, these sorts of concessions are considered effective negotiating strategy.

Buying In A Hurry

THE INVESTOR can sometimes find a good situation for bargaining when the owner must sell quickly to meet the cash requirements of another purchase or is being transferred and wants to get to the new location as quickly as possible.

Transferees usually don't have time to wait around for the best price. They are happy if they take some profit out of a short-term ownership, and they frequently don't concern themselves

Sample Offer To Buy *

To Owner (hereinafter called Seller) _____

Address _____

    The undersigned (hereinafter called Buyer) hereby offers to purchase from Seller the real estate hereinafter described on the terms and conditions herein set forth, if Seller's acceptance of this offer is received by Buyer on or before _____, 19____. Legal description of premises

_____

_____

_____

_____

Street number _____

Size of lot _____

Personal property included _____

_____

Price _____

Deposit herewith (to be returned if offer is not accepted as provided above) _____

_____

Encumbrance deducted _____

_____

_____

Cash to be paid on delivery of deed _____

Balance to be paid as follows: _____

_____

_____

Survey of current date showing no encroachments to be furnished by Seller before closing.

Contract to be held by _____

Closing at office of _____

Deposit to be held by _____

Name of broker _____

Agreement as to commision _____

Date of possession by Buyer _____

LIENS AND ENCUMBRANCES

1. Above mortgage (s) or trust deed (s)
2. Building, building line and use or occupancy restrictions, conditions or covenants of record
3. Easements and party wall agreements
4. General taxes for _____ and subsequent years
5. Installments of special assessments falling due after _____

_____

6. Special assessments for improvements not yet completed
7. Zoning and building laws or ordinances
8. Roads and highways, if any
9. Existing leases as follows (to be assigned to Buyer) _____

_____

Caution: This form is presented for illustrative purposes only. An offer to buy real estate must be very specific, and it usually should be drawn up in consultation with an attorney.

The Process Of Buying

THE FOLLOWING ITEMS ARE TO BE PRO-RATED TO DATE OF DELIVERY OF DEED

1. Interest on encumbrances
2. Insurance premiums (Policies to be assigned to Buyer)
3. General taxes for _____ from
4. Electric light and gas
5. Water taxes
6. Rents
7. Janitor (including vacation allowance)
8. Fuel at market price
9. Any other usual items

TITLE PAPERS

Seller is to furnish within twenty days the following title papers:*

1. A merchantable abstract of title brought down to date hereof.
2. Report of title issued by _____ ,
   brought down to date hereof.
3. A Torrens certificate accompanied by a Torrens title tax search.

*Strike out all but one of 1, 2 and 3.

BASIC CONTRACT PROVISIONS

Buyer agrees to buy said premises at the price stated, and on the terms and subject only to the liens and encumbrances herein stated, and Seller agrees to sell and convey said premises by _____ _____ deed, including the release and waiver of the right of homestead and dower. If the title papers show defects in title not included in the liens and encumbrances referred to above, Seller shall have an additional sixty days within which to cure or remove such defects. When the title papers show that Seller's title is subject only to said liens and encumbrances, Buyer shall within ten days pay the cash to be paid on delivery of deed, at which time the closing shall take place. At the closing Seller shall furnish such A. L. T. A. and other title affidavits as Buyer may reasonably request. Seller may use the proceeds of the sale hereunder to pay and have released encumbrances existing to the time of closing. Upon written notice of either party to the other, the sale hereunder may be closed in escrow, with _____ _____ as escrow agent, and Seller and Buyer shall each pay one-half of the escrow agent's fees. If such defects in title are not cured or removed within the time herein prescribed, Buyer may at his option rescind this contract and have the deposit refunded, whereupon this contract shall become null and void. If prior to delivery of the deed hereunder the improvements on said premises shall be destroyed or materially damaged by fire or other casualty, this contract shall, at the option of Buyer, become null and void. If Buyer defaults in this contract, the deposit is at the option of Seller to be forfeited as liquidated damages, first paying the real estate broker for any expenses incurred and a commission in the amount of _____ per cent of the commission otherwise payable, and rendering the balance to Seller, and the contract shall become null and void. If a report of title is furnished as aforesaid, Seller shall, within fifteen days after closing, furnish an owners title insurance policy in the usual A. L. T. A. form for the full amount of the purchase price. Notices may be served on either party by mail at their said addresses and no tender of deed or purchase money shall be necessary, but a failure to appear upon notice to close at the place mentioned in this contract shall be a default. Time is of the essence of this contract.

Dated _____ , 19____ .

_____ (SEAL)   _____ (SEAL)

_____ (SEAL)   _____ (SEAL)

about pulling top dollar out of the house. What these sellers appreciate is anything the buyer can do to speed up the sale.

When the buyer is the transferee instead of the seller, of course, the advantage is reversed. Generally, the buyer is in the position of weakness, needing to purchase a home in a hurry.

The home investor who is transferred to a new city should take his or her savings with on the first home shopping expedition. By depositing the funds in one or more savings associations that serve areas of interest, the transferee becomes a customer and potentially a borrower for a mortgage loan. This allows the prospective buyer to pick lenders' brains about where property values have been rising fastest, where schools are most respected, where commuting to jobs is easiest, and even where an individual lender would buy if he were in the transferee's situation.

The lender can also give useful advice on how to process the loan as quickly as possible and on finding a good broker, real estate attorney, appraiser, or home inspection expert. This advice can save a great deal of time when the transferee finds a home to purchase. And the lender who is alert to a transferee's need to move quickly will generally do everything possible to expedite a loan application.

Some brokers can be important allies of investors who must buy in a hurry. The broker who has learned the shortcuts that enable his or her client to see the best properties available in the briefest shopping period — then buy and close in the least amount of time — can be extremely valuable. Some brokerage offices operate at a slower pace, generally involving a long period of leading clients around, then by a process of trial and error zeroing in on what the buyer really wants, and finally an unhurried handling of the paperwork. Brokers who regularly service transferees, however, know how to move these procedures along quite rapidly.

The Limits Of Negotiation

IT IS VITAL in buying property that investors know the limits of their ability to handle the costs of ownership. There is much more expense involved than just meeting the mortgage payments, and people coming out of rental apartments (where maintenance and heating and cooling costs were unseen) are sometimes shocked by how much it costs to own a home. Most investors who are paying 25 percent of their gross incomes on the mortgage should figure another 10 percent of the home price on top of that for the other costs of ownership.

"There are two things to keep in mind," says Illinois realtor Joseph Hanauer. "One is that the operating expenses and furnishing costs of a home can inundate you. But you also should figure into your total home expenses the tax benefits that you will receive when you pay your taxes. For a realistic assessment of the costs of ownership, you have to include both factors. Then, buy as much house as you can afford because you will realize more profit from it."

Hanauer also cautions that couples with two incomes should take into account the possibility that one partner might stop working for some reason. "If you are depending on two incomes to buy a home, you should think carefully about

> The expenses of home ownership can overwhelm first-time buyers.

Banks calculate home buying power at 2½ times annual income.

ple in this equation if both husband and wife show a work history of some duration — usually two years or more — and both hold jobs that appear stable.

The following figures represent the buying power of typical middle-income investors following the formula of 2½ times annual income.

Income	Buying Power
$15,000	$37,500
$16,000	$40,000
$17,000	$42,500
$18,000	$45,000
$19,000	$47,500
$20,000	$50,000
$21,000	$52,500
$22,000	$55,000
$23,000	$57,000
$24,000	$60,000
$25,000	$62,500

future plans before entering a commitment that could cause problems later," he warns.

Banks and savings and loan associations generally follow the rule that buyers should not consider purchasing homes more than 2½ times the family's annual income. Buyers who stick to this rule can afford to meet their mortgage payments and keep up their homes. Lenders tend to accept both incomes for a cou-

But these are averages. A buyer who is frugal by nature or in a job where his or her income will increase steadily throughout the term of the loan can often exceed these averages when it comes time to secure a mortgage.

A buyer can also exceed the averages through creative financing. For example, there is a mortgage plan offered in various areas that permits a buyer to borrow in a way that involves relatively small monthly mortgage costs through the first five years of the loan. The mortgage payments increase each year, until after five years the borrower is paying more each month than a fixed-payment loan would have required. Usually, the payments remain constant after the first five years.

This plan is available to people who have higher income expectations each year. The lender feels that by the fifth year, the borrower will be able to handle payments that are higher than the constant payments of a conventional mortgage. This sort of creative financing opens up the housing market to many buyers who would otherwise be excluded, and it allows them to negotiate for a home that the strict law of 2½ times annual income would prohibit them from purchasing.

Arranging Financing

IT IS A mistake to wait until after the residence is chosen to start thinking about financing the home. The prospective borrower for a mortgage loan should already be acquainted with some lender in the area, although not necessarily the one with the biggest ad campaign or most attractive offices. The key characteristic to look for in a lender is flexibility.

The lender should show a willingness to be flexible and not just offer one rigid mortgage plan. He should be willing to negotiate about prepaying the mortgage (i.e., no penalty), accept a second mortgage if the buyer should need one someday, refinance the loan, and make home improvement money available by extending the loan or returning to the original total principal amount without charging full refinancing costs.

The smart home investor looks for more than the lowest interest rate when shopping for financing. A short-term owner, expecting to sell or be transferred after a brief period of time, should pay attention to the number of points involved in closing the deal. For example, a borrower who can get an interest rate of 9.0 percent with a one percent service charge (one point) is usually better off than the person who gets an 8.75 percent interest rate with a two point service charge — provided that the ownership period in both cases will be brief.

The individual who expects to hold property for four years or more should certainly shop for the best interest rate. Sacrificing a point for a quarter of a percent off the interest rate is worthwhile for the borrower who holds a home for four years or more. Of course, the buyer who must struggle to come up with the downpayment wants the smallest number of points possible, and in these circumstances selecting the higher interest rate to save on the number of points would be the smartest strategy.

The individual seeking maximum leverage for the property — i.e., the lowest commitment of personal money and therefore the largest mortgage possible — should seek a lender who will accept private mortgage insurance on a 90 to 95 percent loan. The costs of private mortgage

> For most people,
> the longer
> the mortgage term,
> the better
> the return
> on investment.

insurance are a consideration, but they are partially offset by the higher tax deductions the borrower obtains from the simple act of paying more interest on the loan. Private mortgage insurance can easily be obtained by a buyer with good credit and job security, and many lenders will accept just 5 to 10 percent down if they have assurance from either a private mortgage insurance company or the federal government that the top 5 to 10 percent of their investment will be paid if the buyer defaults.

How much to put down on a house is, of course, a critical investment judgment. The aggressive investor takes the position that the less personal money that goes into an investment the better. For buyers with this bent, zero is a good round number to start with when considering a downpayment. The Veterans Administration will insure some zero downpayment loans for individuals who served in the military and were honorably discharged, and the Federal Housing Administration will insure loans that are close to 100 percent of the purchase price. Many private insurers will lend up to 95 percent of the total amount. With nothing in-

Sample Loan Application

MORTGAGE APPLIED FOR	Type ☐Conv.☐FHA☐VA	Amount $	Interest Rate %	No. of Months	Monthly Payment Principal & Interest $	Escrow/Impounds (to be collected monthly) ☐Taxes ☐Hazard Ins.☐MI ☐
Prepayment Option						

SUBJECT PROPERTY

Property Street Address	City	County	State	Zip	No. Units

Legal Description (Attach description if necessary)	Year Built	Property is: ☐Fee ☐Leasehold ☐Condo ☐PUD ☐DeMinimis PUD

Purpose of Loan: ☐Purchase ☐Construction-Perm. ☐Construction ☐Refinance ☐Other (Explain)

Complete this line if Construction-Perm. or Construction Loan ☞	Lot Value Data Year Acquired _____ $	Original Cost $	Present Value (a) $	Cost of Imps. (b) $	Total (a+b) $	ENTER TOTAL AS PURCHASE PRICE IN DETAILS OF ☐ PURCHASE

Complete this line if a Refinance Loan	Purpose of Refinance	Describe Improvement [ ] made [ ] to be made
Year Acquired	Original Cost	Amt. Existing Liens		Cost: $ _____

Title Will Vest in What Names?	How Will Title Be Held? (Tenancy)

Note Will Be Signed By?	Source of Down Payment and Settlement Charges?

BORROWER				CO-BORROWER*			
Name	Age	Sex**	School Yrs ___	Name	Age	Sex**	School Yrs ___

Present Address No. Years _____ ☐Own ☐Rent	Present Address No. Years _____ ☐Own ☐Rent
Street _____	Street _____
City/State/Zip _____	City/State/Zip _____
Former address if less than 2 years at present address	Former address if less than 2 years at present address
Street _____	Street _____
City/State/Zip _____	City/State/Zip _____
Years at former address ☐Own ☐Rent	Years at former address ☐Own ☐Rent

Marital Status ☐Married Yrs. _____ ☐Unmarried ☐Separated	(Check One)** ☐American Indian ☐Negro/Black	Marital Status ☐Married Yrs. _____ ☐Unmarried ☐Separated	(Check One)** ☐American Indian ☐Negro/Black
Dependents other than Co-Borrower	☐Oriental ☐Spanish American ☐Other Minority ☐White (Non-minority)	Dependents other than listed by Borrower	☐Oriental ☐Spanish American ☐Other Minority ☐White (Non-minority)
Number	Ages		Number	Ages	

Name and Address of Employer	Years employed in this line of work or profession? _____ years Years on this job _____ ☐Self Employed***	Name and Address of Employer	Years employed in this line of work or profession? _____ years Years on this job _____ ☐Self Employed***
Position/Title	Type of Business	Position/Title	Type of Business

GROSS MONTHLY INCOME				MONTHLY HOUSING EXPENSE			DETAILS OF PURCHASE	
Item	Borrower	Co-Borrower	Total		PREVIOUS	PROPOSED		
Base Income	$	$	$	Rent				
Overtime				First Mortgage (P&I)		$	a. Purchase Price	$
Bonuses				Other Financing (P&I)			b. Total Closing Costs	
Commissions				Hazard Insurance			c. Pre Paid Escrows	
Dividends/Interest				Taxes (Real Estate)			d. Total (a + b + c)	$
Net Rental Income				Assessments			e. Amt. This Mortgage	( )
Other [SEE SCHEDULE BELOW]				Mortgage Insurance			f. Other Financing	( )
				Homeowner Assn. Dues			g. Present Equity in Lot	( )
				Total Monthly Pmt	$	$	h. Amt. of Deposit	( )
				Utilities			i. Closing costs paid by Seller	( )
Total	$	$	$	Total	$	$	j. Cash required for closing	$

DESCRIBE OTHER INCOME

B—Borrower C—Co-Borrower NOTE: ALIMONY/CHILD SUPPORT PAYMENTS NEED NOT BE LISTED UNLESS THEIR CONSIDERATION IS DESIRED | Monthly Amt. $

IF EMPLOYED IN CURRENT POSITION FOR LESS THAN TWO YEARS COMPLETE THE FOLLOWING

B/C	Previous Employer/School	City/State	Type of Business	Position/Title	Dates From/To	Monthly Salary
						$

QUESTIONS APPLY TO BOTH BORROWERS

If Yes, explain on attached sheet

	Borrower Yes or No	Co-Borrower Yes or No		Borrower Yes or No	Co-Borrower Yes or No
Have you any outstanding judgments, ever taken bankruptcy, had property foreclosed upon, or given deed in lieu thereof?	___	___	Do you have health and accident insurance?	___	___
			Do you have major medical coverage?	___	___
Co-Maker or endorser on any notes?	___	___	Do you intend to occupy property?	___	___
Defendant/Participant in a Law Suit?	___	___	Will this property be your primary residence?	___	___
Obligated for child support/alimony payments?	___	___	Have you previously owned a home?	___	___
Any portion of the down payment borrowed?	___	___	Value of previously owned home	$ ___	$ ___

*Complete this section and all other co-borrower questions about spouse if the spouse will be jointly obligated with the borrower on the loan or if the borrower is relying on the spouse's income or on community property in obtaining the loan.
**This information is requested only for statistical purposes in accordance with the intent of fair housing law. Furnishing this information is voluntary, but borrowers are urged to do so. No lending decision will be made on the basis of this information or on whether or not it is furnished.
***FHLMC requires self employed to furnish signed copies of one or more most recent Federal Tax Returns or audited Profit and Loss Statements. FNMA requires business credit report, signed Federal Income Tax returns for last two years, and, if available, audited P/L plus balance sheet for same period.

This Statement and any applicable supporting schedules may be completed jointly by both married and unmarried co-borrowers if their assets and liabilities are sufficiently joined so that the Statement can be meaningfully and fairly presented on a combined basis; otherwise separate Statements and Schedules are required (FHLMC 65A/FNMA 1003A). If the co-borrower section was completed about spouse, complete this statement and supporting schedules about spouse also.

☐ Completed Jointly ☐ Not Completed Jointly

STATEMENT OF ASSETS AND LIABILITIES

ASSETS		LIABILITIES AND PLEDGED ASSETS		
Description	Cash or Market Value	Owed To (Name, Address and Account Number)	Mo. Pmt. and Mos. left to pay	Unpaid Balance
Cash Toward Purchase held by		**Indicate by (*) which will be satisfied upon sale or upon refinancing of subject property.**		
		Installment Debt (include "revolving" charge accounts)	$ Pmt./Mos. /	$
Checking and Savings Accounts (Indicate names of Institutions/Acct. Nos.)			/	
			/	
			/	
Stocks and Bonds (No./description)			/	
			/	
Life Insurance Net Cash Value *Face Amount ($*		Automobile Loan		
SUBTOTAL LIQUID ASSETS			/	
Real Estate Owned (Enter Total Market Value from Real Estate Schedule)		Real Estate Loans (Itemize and Identify Lender)		
Vested Interest in Retirement Fund				
Net Worth of Business Owned (ATTACH FINANCIAL STATEMENT)				
Auto (Make and Year)		Other Debt Including Stock Pledges (Itemize)		
			/	
Furniture and Personal Property		Alimony and Child Support Payments		
Other Assets (Itemize)			/	
		TOTAL MONTHLY PAYMENTS	$	
TOTAL ASSETS	A. $	NET WORTH (A.–B.) $	TOTAL LIABILITIES	B. $

SCHEDULE OF REAL ESTATE OWNED (If Additional Properties Owned Attach Separate Schedule)

Address of Property (Indicate S if Sold, PS if Pending Sale or R if Rental being held for income)	Type of Property	Present Market Value	Amount of Mortgages & Liens	Gross Rental Income	Mortgage Payments	Taxes, Ins. Maintenance and Misc.	Net Rental Income
TOTALS →							

LIST PREVIOUS CREDIT REFERENCES

B—Borrower C—Co-Borrower	Owed To (Name and Address)	Account Number	Purpose	Highest Balance	Date Paid
				$	

AGREEMENT: The undersigned hereby applies for the loan described herein to be secured by a first mortgage or trust deed on the property described herein and represents that no part of said premises will be used for any purpose forbidden by law or restriction and that all statements made in this application are true and made for the purpose of obtaining the loan. Verification may be obtained from any source named herein. The original or a copy of this application will be retained by the lender even if the loan is not granted.

I fully understand that it is a federal crime punishable by fine or imprisonment or both to knowingly make any false statements concerning any of the above facts, as applicable under the provisions of Title 18, United States Code, Section 1014.

Signature (Borrower)_____ Date_____ Signature (Co-Borrower)_____ Date_____

Home Phone _____ Business Phone _____ Home Phone _____ Business Phone _____

The Federal Equal Credit Opportunity Act prohibits creditors from discriminating against credit applicants on the basis of sex or marital status. The Federal Agency which administers compliance with this law concerning this savings and loan association is the Federal Home Loan Bank Board, 320 First Street N.W., Washington, D.C. 20552 (local office, 111 East Wacker Drive, Chicago, Illinois 60601).

Additionally the Federal Fair Housing Act also prohibits discrimination on the basis of race, color, religion, sex or national origin.

I/We have received a copy of the Equal Credit Opportunity Notice and the booklet entitled, "Settlement Costs and You". Yes ☐ No ☐

FOR LENDER'S USE ONLY

(FNMA REQUIREMENT ONLY) This application was taken by _____, a full time employee of
Interviewer

_____, in a face to face interview with the prospective borrower.
(Name of Lender)

THE UNDERSIGNED OFFICER HAS APPROVED THIS APPLICATION FOR A LOAN OF $_____ @ _____ %

INTEREST PER ANNUM FOR A TERM OF _____ YEARS WITH A $_____COMMITMENT FEE AND A $_____SERVICE CHARGE.

OFFICER_____DATE_____

APPROVAL ADVISED_____DATE_____AUDITED BY_____

vested, the buyer stands to make a 100 percent profit on any appreciation in value that the property enjoys.

Conventional mortgage lenders are not the only source of mortgage funds, however. The seller is an often overlooked source who may well be willing to hold the mortgage on his or her old home at the full amount of its value while charging a slightly lower interest rate than the mortgage lenders demand.

Sellers who don't intend to buy another residence are especially good prospects for financing. They don't need the full proceeds of a sale for a downpayment on a new home, and they often would prefer to defer their tax liability through gradual receipt of payment of the purchase price. Of course, these sellers are also attracted to the idea of receiving a greater return on their property than they would receive by putting the one-time proceeds of a sale into a savings account.

Sometimes, the best place to turn is to an individual other than the seller. A relative or friend with a great deal of cash that is sitting unproductively in the stock market or gathering comparatively little return in a savings account might find a mortgage to be an attractive investment. Credit unions represent another source for home loans; their rates usually are lower than a savings institution's because their purpose is to serve a select group of employees or members of an organization.

The Mortgage Term

WHEN DECIDING HOW long a mortgage to take, the buyer should make some sort of estimate as to how long he or she intends to hold the property. A person looking at a two-year holding period followed by a job transfer should make different decisions about financing than the person who expects to live in a home for five or ten years.

Nonetheless, it almost always works better for the investor to seek the longest mortgage term available — a term of 30 years or more to repay is better than a term of 20 or 25 years. Some government-insured loans provide for a 35-year repayment period, but it is more common to obtain a 30-year loan.

In the United States, most people move about every five years. Changes in lifestyle or job or marital or economic status make it very unlikely that anyone will live in a home for the full mortgage term. Since the lower the personal financial commitment at the time of sale, the better the investment, the longer term mortgages lead to better profit ratios.

True, a 20- or 25-year term will accumulate equity more rapidly and save a considerable amount of interest compared to a 30-year loan. But to realize these benefits, the owner should hold the property for most or all of the term. Selling a home in 10 years or less diminishes the benefits of the shorter term because the investor's money is not well leveraged. More personal money is put into the property, thereby reducing the percentage of return on the investment.

Assume that two home investors have purchased similar properties with $40,000 mortgages at identical 8.5 percent interest rates. One takes a 30-year mortgage and the other a 20-year mortgage. The owner with the 30-year loan pays $3,691 a year in principal and interest payments, while the owner with the 20-year loan pays $4,126 a year.

Both sell after five years. The owner with the 30-year mortgage is $2,175 ahead because he has paid that much less in monthly mortgage payments, He has also deducted more from his federal income taxes due to the higher interest payments.

On the other hand, the owner with the 20-year mortgage term has put an additional $700 in equity into the property, which he now gets back at resale. But he has committed more of his own money to the property and thus realized a lower percentage return than has the 30-year borrower who committed less of his own money and more of the lender's. The whole object of a good investment, of course, is to maximize the return on a minimum out-of-pocket expense.

In summary, the smart home investor uses a lender to full advantage. Among the services which a good lender can provide to help maximize an investor's return on a real estate investment are the following:

- Assistance in finding experts such as appraisers, home inspectors, and attorneys.

- Advice on neighborhoods, trends in value, and reputation of builders.

- Lowest interest rate with fewest number of points.

- Lowest downpayment.

- Longest mortgage term.

Closing The Deal

The Process Of Buying

UNFORTUNATELY, THE final step in the process of buying does not lend itself to great savings. In fact, it may not even be worth the effort for a buyer to go beyond a reasonable evaluation of the charges that the lender is required to estimate prior to closing.

In 1976 Congress enacted a law entitled the Real Estate Settlement Procedures Act (RESPA) that was designed to take the shock out of closing costs by giving buyers an advance look at how much additional capital they would need to complete a real estate purchase. Congress assumed that — armed with this information — buyers could shop around for better terms, but Congress failed to realize that most closing costs are fixed and there is no way to lower them. For the prorated share of annual property taxes, the cost of title insurance, the points the lender charges to make the loan, the costs of legal counsel, and the initial insurance payments, the buyer of a $40,000 home can expect to pay $1,000 to $1,500 and will find few ways to reduce that expenditure.

If the Real Estate Settlement Procedures Act has accomplished anything, it has helped end the practice of brokers receiving kickbacks from attorneys for referred business. The attorney, of course, should have the interests of the client foremost at closing, rather than the interests of the broker who has sent the business. The attorney is the client's adviser as to whether closing costs, as estimated by the lender, are fair and reasonable. If the attorney feels that the costs are excessive, the home investor should be encouraged to challenge the charges or to shop around for better value. As previously stated, however, such shopping is generally futile.

The way a buyer takes title to the property can be extremely important, and in this respect an attorney's advice can definitely result in long-term savings. Joint tenancy is one way to take title, and it is probably the most common way for a married couple. In joint tenancy, two or more owners hold undivided title to the property. The surviving owner (or owners) automatically receives the share of another owner who dies; as a result, the property does not get involved in probate of the decedent's estate.

In some states, the property purchaser can use a land trust, which means putting title to the property into the hands of a trustee (usually a bank). A trust agreement specifically designates the benefits of ownership to the buyer of the property, and the buyer's beneficiary can sell those interests, borrow against them, or convey part or all of them to someone else.

Either of these approaches to taking title avoids the long process of probate in the event of an owner's death, but they are not necessarily better than simple separate ownership of the title. They may, in fact, lead to problems in some states. For example, some states allow one owner in joint tenancy to convey his or her share of the property to someone else without the knowledge of the other owner or owners. Thus, a wife and mistress of a deceased man may end up as joint owners of a home if the decedent transferred his interest to the mistress before he died. Other states require that the spouse consent to conveyance of his or her partner's interest.

Due to the complexities involved in this decision — notably the buyer's age, tax bracket, and marital status — plus the differences in state law, the question of how to take title is a subject that is well worth pursuing with an attorney and tax adviser.

RESPA
generally
has failed
to help
investors lower
closing costs.

Sample RESPA Statement Of Closing Costs

A. U.S. DEPARTMENT OF HOUSING AND URBAN DEVELOPMENT SETTLEMENT STATEMENT	B. TYPE OF LOAN
	1. ☐ FHA 2. ☐ FMHA 3. ☐ CONV. UNINS.
	4. ☐ VA 5. ☐ CONV. INS.
	6. FILE NUMBER: 7. LOAN NUMBER:
	8. MORT. INS. CASE NO.:

C. NOTE: This form is furnished to give you a statement of actual settlement costs. Amounts paid to and by the settlement agent are shown. Items marked "(p.o.c.)" were paid outside the closing; they are shown here for informational purposes and are not included in the totals.

D. NAME OF BORROWER:	E. NAME OF SELLER:	F. NAME OF LENDER:

G. PROPERTY LOCATION:	H. SETTLEMENT AGENT:	I. SETTLEMENT DATE:
	PLACE OF SETTLEMENT:	

J. SUMMARY OF BORROWER'S TRANSACTION:		K. SUMMARY OF SELLER'S TRANSACTION:	
100. **GROSS AMOUNT DUE FROM BORROWER**		400. **GROSS AMOUNT DUE TO SELLER**	
101. Contract sales price		401. Contract sales price	
102. Personal property		402. Personal property	
103. Settlement charges to borrower (line 1400)		403.	
104.		404.	
105.		405.	
Adjustments for items paid by seller in advance		Adjustments for items paid by seller in advance	
106. City/town taxes to		406. City/town taxes to	
107. County taxes to		407. County taxes to	
108. Assessments to		408. Assessments to	
109.		409.	
110.		410.	
111.		411.	
112.		412.	
120. **GROSS AMOUNT DUE FROM BORROWER**		420. **GROSS AMOUNT DUE TO SELLER**	
200. **AMOUNTS PAID BY OR IN BEHALF OF BORROWER**		500. **REDUCTIONS IN AMOUNT DUE TO SELLER**	
201. Deposit or earnest money		501. Excess deposit (see Instructions)	
202. Principal amount of new loan(s)		502. Settlement charges to seller (line 1400)	
203. Existing loan(s) taken subject to		503. Existing loan(s) taken subject to	
204.		504. Payoff of first mortgage loan	
205.		505. Payoff of second mortgage loan	
206.		506.	
207.		507.	
208.		508.	
209.		509.	
Adjustments for items unpaid by seller		Adjustments for items unpaid by seller	
210. City/town taxes to		510. City/town taxes to	
211. County taxes to		511. County taxes to	
212. Assessments to		512. Assessments to	
213.		513.	
214.		514.	
215.		515.	
216.		516.	
217.		517.	
218.		518.	
219.		519.	
220. **TOTAL PAID BY/FOR BORROWER**		520. **TOTAL REDUCTION AMOUNT DUE SELLER**	
300. **CASH AT SETTLEMENT FROM OR TO BORROWER**		600. **CASH AT SETTLEMENT TO OR FROM SELLER**	
301. Gross amount due from borrower (line 120)		601. Gross amount due to seller (line 420)	
302. Less amounts paid by/for borrower (line 220)	( )	602. Less reduction amount due seller (line 520)	( )
303. **CASH (☐ FROM) (☐ TO) BORROWER**		603. **CASH (☐ TO) (☐ FROM) SELLER**	

U.S. DEPARTMENT OF HOUSING AND URBAN DEVELOPMENT
SETTLEMENT STATEMENT
PAGE 2

L. SETTLEMENT CHARGES		PAID FROM BORROWER'S FUNDS AT SETTLEMENT	PAID FROM SELLER'S FUNDS AT SETTLEMENT
700.	TOTAL SALES/BROKER'S COMMISSION based on price $ @ % =		
	Division of commission (line 700) as follows:		
701.	$ to		
702.	$ to		
703.	Commission paid at Settlement		
704.			
800.	ITEMS PAYABLE IN CONNECTION WITH LOAN		
801.	Loan Origination Fee %		
802.	Loan Discount %		
803.	Appraisal Fee to		
804.	Credit Report to		
805.	Lender's Inspection Fee		
806.	Mortgage Insurance Application Fee to		
807.	Assumption Fee		
808.			
809.			
810.			
811.			
900.	ITEMS REQUIRED BY LENDER TO BE PAID IN ADVANCE		
901.	Interest from to @ $ /day		
902.	Mortgage Insurance Premium for mo. to		
903.	Hazard Insurance Premium for yrs. to		
904.	yrs. to		
905.			
1000.	RESERVES DEPOSITED WITH LENDER FOR		
1001.	Hazard insurance mo. @ $ /mo.		
1002.	Mortgage insurance mo. @ $ /mo.		
1003.	City property taxes mo. @ $ /mo.		
1004.	County property taxes mo. @ $ /mo.		
1005.	Annual assessments mo. @ $ /mo.		
1006.	mo. @ $ /mo.		
1007.	mo. @ $ /mo.		
1008.	mo. @ $ /mo.		
1100.	TITLE CHARGES		
1101.	Settlement or closing fee to		
1102.	Abstract or title search to		
1103.	Title examination to		
1104.	Title insurance binder to		
1105.	Document preparation to		
1106.	Notary fees to		
1107.	Attorney's fees to		
	(includes above items No.:		
1108.	Title insurance to		
	(includes above items No.:		
1109.	Lender's coverage $		
1110.	Owner's coverage $		
1111.			
1112.			
1113.			
1200.	GOVERNMENT RECORDING AND TRANSFER CHARGES		
1201.	Recording fees: Deed $; Mortgage $; Releases $		
1202.	City/county tax/stamps: Deed $; Mortgage $		
1203.	State tax/stamps: Deed $; Mortgage $		
1204.			
1205.			
1300.	ADDITIONAL SETTLEMENT CHARGES		
1301.	Survey to		
1302.	Pest inspection to		
1303.			
1304.			
1305.			
1400.	TOTAL SETTLEMENT CHARGES (enter on lines 103 and 502, Sections J and K)		

The Undersigned Acknowledges Receipt of This Settlement Statement and Agrees to the Correctness Thereof.

_____   _____
     Buyer   **Seller**

Insuring The New Home

A HOMEOWNER IS required by the lender to have an insurance policy that protects at least against fire loss. In fact, many mortgage lenders collect the premium for such a policy on a monthly basis along with the principal, interest, and tax payments.

It definitely pays to shop for the best insurance policy, but not necessarily the cheapest. The lending institution can be a good place to start shopping. Many savings associations have their own insurance subsidiaries, and although they may or may not offer the best rates, they certainly are concerned with seeing that their customers are covered adequately so that no one will suffer excessively in the event of a loss.

The home investor should inquire about the type and amount of coverage needed. Many lenders push liability insurance because homeowners are so frequently sued by someone injured on the property, and the awards in some of these cases have been astronomical. Since the annual cost of boosting the personal liability portion of a homeowners policy from $25,000 to $100,000 coverage amounts to only about $5 to $8, owners should make certain that they are adequately protected. Even going to $300,000 may be justified for the small increase in premium involved.

Burglary rates have also been soaring, and smart homeowners carry more coverage on the goods in their homes than they did formerly. It is especially important to have a rider (or, as the insurance industry calls it, a floater) that covers expensive items such as jewelry, furs, and fine art. These items may not be protected to full value by a standard homeowners policy, and it is worth the higher premium one must pay to protect one's investment in such costly goods.

Full value means exact replacement of whatever is lost. Unless an owner carries insurance equivalent to 80 percent of the value of the building, however, he or she will not receive full value in the event that the home is destroyed. That 80 percent figure doesn't include land, of course, because land can't be destroyed or damaged, and some policies also allow an ex-

> Home insurance must be upgraded annually to retain full value coverage.

clusion for the foundation of a house which is rarely damaged in a fire.

In figuring insurance costs, companies use the rule-of-thumb that the land represents 20 percent of the value and the foundation 5 percent. Full value coverage amounts to 80 percent of the remainder. Thus, on a $40,000 house, 20 percent for the land is $8,000 and 5 percent for the foundation equals another $2,000, leaving $30,000 in insurable value; an owner should insure 80 percent of that amount, or $24,000.

Homeowners whose property has appreciated 10 to 15 percent every year often forget to increase their insurance in order to maintain 80 percent or full value coverage. When a fire occurs, these owners get some percentage of the total claim, but they receive only the depreciated replacement cost based on an insurance industry formula.

To get an idea of what 80 percent of their current home value amounts to, owners should size up their property in terms of comparable properties that have been sold recently. An insurance agent can confirm the correctness of the appraisal, and most good insurance companies make certain that their clients are aware of needed increases in coverage. Some companies have an automatic review procedure, while others have an automatic escalation clause based on value trends in the area. It is important to check with one's agent as to how value increases will be handled to protect the home against falling below the 80 percent level.

An investor who has chosen a home for a renovation effort might find insurance hard to obtain. Insurance company "redlining" — the denial of insurance to certain high risk areas — is a documented fact, affecting neighborhoods where the insurers have not recognized or accepted a reverse from decline to upgrading. Investors in these areas who cannot obtain insurance should investigate federal crime insurance and a state administered program called Fair Access to Insurance Requirements (FAIR) by contacting the state insurance director.

Since there are 500,000 agents in the United States representing 3,000 insurance companies, picking the right one can be confusing. Yet choosing an agency and company for a homeowners policy should be done carefully. It would be well for the person seeking insurance to try three sources: the agency associated with the lending institution (if there is one), local "captive" agencies (those operated by the very large insurance companies), and an independent broker or agent who has access to a number of insurance companies.

Best's Insurance Guide, a guide to the reputation of insurance companies, is available at most public libraries. It provides a starting point for insurance buyers by indicating the quality of every company a homeowner is likely to consider. After finding companies with good reputations, the owner must then decide what should be covered and how much the coverage will cost under each plan offered by a reputable insurer.

Homeowners Policies

THE FOUR HOMEOWNERS policies that most insurance companies offer include the basic form, or HO-1 policy, that covers damages from fire or lightning; windstorm or hail; explosion; riot or civil commotion; aircraft or vehicles; smoke; loss of property removed from an endangered premises; vandalism and malicious mischief; theft; and glass breakage.

Such a policy may be enough coverage for many people. It is certainly the least expensive homeowners policy available. The next cheapest is the HO-2, which adds coverage against falling objects; weight of ice, snow, and sleet; collapse of a building; damage from a hot water heating system or to appliances designed for heating water; overflow of water or steam in a plumbing or air conditioning system; freezing of plumbing, heating, and air conditioning systems; and injury from electrical appliances, fixtures, and wiring.

The HO-2 policy would be more appropriate in northern regions than in warm weather states because the likelihood of damage from most listed items would be higher in the cold weather areas. The HO-3 policy covers a few more perils, and HO-5 — the most expensive — covers every peril except flood, earthquake, war, and nuclear attack. An HO-4 policy just covers personal property and is intended for apartment dwellers.

Several factors affect the price of a homeowners policy. One is the deductible clause, which requires the homeowner to pay the first $50 or $100 of the cost of repairing any insured damage to the property. If the owner increases the deductible, the savings in premium costs can be substantial.

Brick homes command a lower insurance premium from most companies than do frame homes, primarily due to the risk of fire damage. It should be noted, however, that the fire code rating of a community also affects the cost of homeowners insurance. This rating can change as the community modernizes its fire department, goes to full-time rather than voluntary fire protection, provides a good system of fire hydrants, etc. A smoke detector installed in a home may also lead to a reduced homeowners insurance premium.

The key to buying homeowners insurance is to have enough protection but not too much. Most policies exclude replacement of motorized vehicles, animals, rented items, and some business-related property; if these items are important, an owner can usually get insurance coverage to protect them. Certainly extra insurance is needed in flood-prone or earthquake-prone areas, and homes with special features like expensive lighting fixtures should be covered to the amount of their value.

Protecting The Home Investment

*I*T SHOULD BE the home investor's goal to have sufficient insurance to cover all items of substantial value and all potential perils without paying for unnecessary protection. The following list includes those items and perils that are not usually found in a standard homeowner's policy; by checking the blanks that correspond to needed coverage and then showing the list to three insurers for estimates on the additional protection, homeowners can assure themselves of getting complete coverage at a fair price.

Item	Protection Needed
$100,000 in liability	_____
$300,000 in liability	_____
Flood	_____
Earthquake	_____
Landslide	_____
Water backup in sewers or drains	_____
Below-surface water damage	_____
Damage to wharf or dock	_____
Damage to heating or cooling equipment caused by power loss	_____
Sidewalk buckling caused by freezing and thaw	_____

Roof collapse caused by weight of ice or snow	_____
Loss of:	
Currency (amount)	_____
Manuscript	_____
Motorized vehicles (autos, snowmobiles, minibikes)	_____
Outdoor antennas	_____
Patio furniture	_____
Outdoor carpeting	_____
Awnings	_____
Trees, shrubs, lawn	_____
Securities or bank notes	_____
Jewelry, gems, precious stones	_____
Furs	_____
Stamp or coin collections	_____
Watercraft or trailers	_____
Animals, birds, or fish	_____
Fences, driveways, walks	_____
Credit cards	_____

It pays to be ready to prove an insurance claim. One of the best ways is to take some photos of the insured property — inexpensive photos of every wall in every room — and put them somewhere outside the home for safekeeping. When a claim has to be made, these pictures will show exactly what the property looked like before it was damaged. Along with pictures, owners should also supply insurance companies with evidence of ownership of the property — i.e., the proof of title provided at closing by a title insurance company. They should also request that the insurance companies certify in writing that the evidence supplied is acceptable.

In some cases, insurance companies have delayed payment on a claim for a considerable length of time because they maintained that they did not have clear evidence that the insured actually owned the property. Although not a valid reason in most cases to deny or delay payment, insurance companies do this all too frequently for homeowners to ignore the possibility. Once a company concedes in writing that it knows of the owner's title to the property, one source of potential conflict is eliminated.

Another lengthy delay can occur, however, if the insurer insists that a complicated set of forms and procedures be completed with every claim. In fact, owners should question insurance companies about their claim procedures and make the answer — obtained in writing — an important consideration in choosing an insuring company. Too many consumers have discovered that following a serious fire or other severe damage that the insurance companies caused unnecessary delay and expense in adjusting the claim.

Mortgage Life Insurance

ANOTHER FORM OF insurance that lending institutions often suggest is mortgage life insurance which pays off the mortgage in the event of the borrower's death. Lenders point out that the incidence of death of a borrower during a mortgage term is much greater than the inci-

dence of fire, yet many more owners carry fire insurance than carry mortgage life insurance.

The wisdom in carrying mortgage life insurance depends on the age of the borrower and the length of time he or she expects to hold the property. Although actuaries point out that the incidence of death of a 25-year-old borrower over the term of a 25-year mortgage is one in twelve, that 25-year-old borrower is likely to change homes three to five times in 25 years and will not pay off the mortgage on a single home.

In most cases, the appreciated value of the home should be adequate security in the event of a borrower's death, and thus mortgage life insurance generally represents an unnecessary expense. But circumstances vary as to the borrower's age and health, the ability of survivors to continue mortgage payments, and the length of time the investor expects to hold the property before selling it.

Ideal Insurance Coverage

THE IDEAL INSURANCE policy would protect the homeowner against all the hazards of the basic or HO-1 policy, plus $100,000 or more of personal liability, plus any perils that frequently occur in the area (e.g., damage from the weight of ice and snow or from burst water pipes in the far north and from tornados in some areas of the midwest. The policy would provide living expenses in case the home is damaged by fire or other disaster, and it would cover the full replacement cost of personal property that might be stolen or damaged.

The way to go about buying such a policy is to interview three agents, ask them to submit a written price for these areas of coverage (specifying, of course, the insurance company that will be providing the coverage), and then make a choice. The choice should be based on a combination of price, the reputation of the insuring company, and the owner's personal evaluation of the agent; information about the agent's services from someone who has had a claim processed by the agency is most helpful in making this evaluation.

Paying Real Estate Taxes

REAL ESTATE TAXES represent another area of expenditure — and of potential saving — for the home buyer. Tax savings can be accomplished both by purchasing a home in an area with low and stable assessment rates and by appealing the assessment when the homeowner can prove that his or her taxes are too high. Sometimes, in fact, it is not even necessary to prove that the tax is too high; the simple act of protesting a real estate tax levy often results in a reduction.

Real estate taxes are figured in what is basically a two-step process. First, an appraiser employed by the city or county assessor's office makes an estimate of the value of every property in a community. Then the assessor converts the appraised value (or market value) to assessed value by multiplying the figure by whatever assessment ratio the community utilizes; frequently the ratio is 30 to 50 percent rather than the full 100 percent of market value.

Protesters generally get their property taxes lowered.

This process is actually a political gimmick, contrived to make homeowners feel that they are receiving a break by the assessor not taxing them on the full current value of their property. It is only a gimmick, however; every real estate owner is expected to pay a fair share of community services as budgeted each year by the local government and school district.

The point to remember is that the fairness of an assessment does not relate to the market value of the property. It relates to the assessment placed on comparable real estate, and an assessment that is out of line with others merits complaint and adjustment.

Property taxes should be one major consideration for a prospective buyer. Usually, taxes are lower in stable, older communities where the schools have been built, the curbs and sidewalks constructed, and the recreational facilities and parks established. Communities with a substantial number of industrial and commercial areas (such as shopping centers) also offer lower tax rates. In many cases these facilities contribute more than their share to local taxes because they are taxed at a higher rate than homes. Thus, the homeowner is taxed less to run the community because somebody else — the businessman in the tax district — is paying part of the owner's share. A call to the assessor's office will elicit both the ratio of assessed value to market value and the tax rate.

Two $40,000 homes, for example, can be assessed quite differently, at 50 percent of market value in the one instance and at only 30 percent in the other. The tax would be collected on a $20,000 assessed value in the 50 percent district and on $12,000 assessed value in the 30 percent community. Since the tax rate might be only $40 per thousand in the 50 percent district and $80 per thousand in the 30 percent district, however, the actual tax bill in the first case would be $800 a year (20 — representing $20,000 — times $40) while in the second it would be $960 (12 — representing $12,000 — times $80) per annum. Thus, it is possible for an owner to pay higher taxes in a community with a lower ratio of assessed value to market value.

Protesting Property Taxes

IN THE PROCESS of buying a home or immediately afterward the owner should make certain that his or her tax assessment vis-a-vis other homes in the community is appropriate. The assessment role — available to the public at the assessor's office — consists of a series of cards or a computer printout showing the assessed value of every property in a community. By comparing the information about similar properties and the one recently purchased, the homeowner can determine whether he or she is being taxed fairly. If the assessments on similar homes are lower by 10 percent or more, then he or she has good reason to appeal.

In most cases, assessors prepare a tentative roll of annual assessments that is available for inspection by the taxpayer for a certain period during which assessments may be challenged. The smart home investor learns what dates that roll is open and checks his or her own assessment against the comparable properties every year. If the rise in other owners' assessments does not keep pace, the investor has good cause to seek a review.

This review — first with the assessor's office, then with a review board if the investor fails to get satisfaction — requires that the owner be able to show that the assessor's office has undervalued other real estate in relationship to his or her own. If there is any substance to such a claim, the odds are that the investor's overassessment will be rectified. In fact, according to national studies, almost every appealed assessment is reduced. The assessor — shown reasonable evidence — generally makes an adjustment and avoids the hassle of going to the assessment review board.

If the assessor balks, however, the owner must appear before the review board, often with an official complaint filed on a special form developed by the board or the state to simplify and expedite appeals. The owner must show all evidence to support a claim at this time. This evidence should consist of something in the nature of an appraisal or a bill of sale if the property was recently purchased, and the assessments on comparable properties as gathered from the assessment roll.

An owner has nothing to lose by an appeal if there is a shred of convincing evidence available. A claim that one is being treated unequally in relationship to other property owners may well be supported by the facts. It has been estimated that as many as 20 million property owners are overassessed, and the home investor who can show that he or she is one of those 20 million can profit substantially by filing a complaint and — if necessary — an appeal.

Do~It~Yourself Property Appraising

THERE IS NO great mystery involved in appraising real estate, and anyone can figure out what price a given property should bring within the acceptable limits — high or low — of about 10 percent.

Professional appraisers almost always arrive at their home valuations by comparing a house for sale with similar properties that have been sold recently in similar neighborhoods. Adjustments for the presence or absence of particular amenities in the home are relatively easy to make, and, of course, some adjustment must be made if values have appreciated at an unusually rapid rate in the area since sales of comparable properties were completed.

Formerly, appraisers used three methods in determining a home's value. They used the market approach involving comparison of similar properties — always considered the most reliable method. Then, they computed the cost of replacing the house from scratch, subtracting the loss of value to a new home due to wear and tear. Finally, they estimated how much rent the home would bring and what income that rent would produce after expenses; they then multiplied the latter figure by a factor based on what someone buying the home to rent it out would consider an adequate return on investment.

Recently, however, appraisers have concluded that the only approach to home valuation that makes sense is a comparison with similar properties that have actually been negotiated in the market by informed buyers and sellers. The appraisers consider only those transactions in which the buyer and seller were not related, where no special financing terms were offered, and where no other special situations existed that might have influenced the purchase price.

To do a personal appraisal of a home that one intends to buy or sell — a professional appraisal can run from $100 to $200 — the home investor needs a good deal of authentic data. Neighborhood rumor of what someone sold a home for is not sufficient. Fortunately, two excellent sources of information are readily available: real estate agents and the public records.

The quickest and easiest source to tap for home prices in the neighborhood is the real estate agent. A broker maintains a file of listing cards arranged by price, and by scanning these cards quickly, the home investor should be able to find a house that looks like or meets the same description as the property under consideration. The broker's cards showing recent sales are more informative than the ones showing current listings because an actual sale price does not include some seller's inflated idea of what his or her property will bring.

A single property really does not provide enough data for a solid appraisal. A single sale could have been influenced by special circumstances that have no bearing on the present property. A series of sales, usually three or more, tell what is happening in the market.

After obtaining this sort of data, the home investor must start making adjustments. When

A value comparison with similar properties sold recently in the open market is the most reliable and accurate method of home appraisal.

it comes to predicting how much extra buyers will pay for better-than-average insulation or location or landscaping, etc., even the professional appraisers must rely on educated guesses. They again go back to comparing properties as similar to each other as possible in order to minimize the subjective factor, and that's about all a do-it-yourself appraiser can do. Actually, it is rather easy to establish how much extra the market will pay for central air conditioning or a two-car garage by comparing similar properties that sold with and without these amenities.

The easiest properties to appraise are condominium or cooperative units where the price per square foot makes it simple to compare units in comparable buildings or townhouse developments. The amenities are generally identical or nearly so, making few adjustments, if any, necessary.

The most difficult homes for the do-it-yourselfer to appraise are the custom-built

City hall
offers a wealth
of information
for the industrious
and tactful
do-it-yourself
appraiser.

older houses. Since each one is essentially a unique entity, the comparative method is not as reliable as it is when appraising newer, more standardized properties.

It is vital to making a sound investment in an older home, though, to know something about the life it has led. Much of the information needed can be found at local government offices, especially at the city or village hall and the tax assessor's office. It may take a few hours to dig out the relevant data, but the search could result in thousands of dollars in a buyer's or seller's pocket.

To get the necessary information, the do-it-yourselfer needs the cooperation of local civil servants. Although providing help is part of their job and they should do it without making an issue, their cooperation may have to be cultivated by a bit of extra courtesy.

The tax assessor's office has much of the information — i.e., the price for which the property last sold and the improvements that have been made over the years — needed to appraise the home accurately. Records will indicate how much the property was last appraised for by the county or local assessor's appraiser. Frequently, however, the amount shown will seem much too low. The explanation for this low figure lies in the fact that it must be divided by the assessment tax ratio, which can vary from 20 to 100 percent of the assessed value. To learn how much the property is really worth to the assessor, one must obtain the tax ratio and divide the assessed value by that number. For example, property assessed at $20,000 with a 69 percent tax ratio is actually worth $28,985 ($20,000 divided by 69).

Since assessments are at least a year behind increases in property values (it takes the assessor a year or more to appraise all the homes in his jurisdiction), however, even the properly computed assessed value is not an accurate gauge to what the property is worth today; it indicates no more than the bottom end of the range. It can be a valuable figure, nonetheless, in that it allows for a comparison with homes that are similar in size and type to see whether the property in question is assessed equally and fairly.

The assessor also has records as to when the home was built, its physical description (square footage, etc.), and other details. In larger communities, this information may be computerized and available at the touch of a clerk's finger, or — where the technology is less advanced — it may be found on the same sheet as the valuation. Generally, the person in search of the data described needs key numbers for the properties to be investigated; books of addresses and key numbers are located in the assessor's office.

The key number also comes in handy when seeking the ownership history of the house. Somewhere in city hall is a chronological list of the ownership, purchase price, type of deed conveyed, size of the mortgage, and the lender's name for each mortgage placed on the property.

Instead of dollar amounts, the purchase price may be represented by tax stamps for each sale. The stamps necessitate a bit of extra work in order to find out the selling price in each transaction involving the property. Usually, the local government requires the buyer to pay $1 or more for tax stamps per $1,000 in purchase price when a property changes hands. Simply a revenue-producing device, the tax stamps nevertheless provide useful data in the public records as to the price at which a home was sold. Although in some communities it is possible to buy more stamps than needed as a device to conceal the purchase price, in most cases buyers pay only for the appropriate number of tax stamps.

One of the most productive offices for the home investor to visit when trying to find information about a property is the building inspector's office. The inspection files on the property, obtainable with the address or key number, provide important information on significant work done to the home over the years. Plumbing, electrical, and structural alterations are included, along with data regarding when the home was built, who built it, and how much it cost to build. This information can prove valuable to a buyer as a check against claims the owner may make concerning improvements or additions to the property.

> Appraising can never be an exact science, but any home investor can learn how to place a reasonably accurate price on residential property.

The home investor also should visit the zoning and planning commission to learn what is happening in the area. If something out of character to a neighborhood gets approval, it can damage values severely. A check of the zoning for any vacant land nearby will reveal whether anything — e.g., a highrise apartment building, shopping center, etc. — going into that space might adversely affect the desirability of the residential property.

Almost everything that happens to residential property becomes a part of the public records, records to which any taxpayer has access. In fact, professional appraisers get much of their information from these records, too.

As most appraisers willingly admit, appraising property is not an exact science. It is a judgment business based on day-to-day acquaintance with the market. A home investor can approximate that knowledge by making reasonable comparisons among similar homes and backing educated guesses with whatever hard data can be found.

Real Estate Record Keeping

THE PERSON WHO makes money on real estate is generally the person who knows how to maximize the tax deductions which the government allows on residential property. The Internal Revenue Service, however, requires that homeowners be able to verify those items claimed as tax deductions with records of past transactions. Obviously, few homeowners retain every record relating to their homes for their entire period of ownership. Therefore, the question arises: What kind of records to keep and for how long?

"Receipts and cancelled checks are what you want to show," says Howard Lapin, an agent of the Internal Revenue Service. "Each case is a little different and each agent might require a little different standard. But if the records are in good shape, you shouldn't have too much of a problem."

The IRS statute of limitations concerning deductions for home expenses extends to just three years. In other words, a homeowner faces little chance of being called in to explain and verify tax deductions relating to the home after more than three years following the claims.

Lapin suggests, however, that owners hold records beyond the usual three years if the home is being rented out to someone else. "If you put on a new roof or buy appliances or do any major renovation on a home you are rent-ing to someone, keep all the records of your costs. You will have to set up a schedule for some improvements or replacements, meaning that you can only deduct a percentage of their cost each year rather than deduct the whole cost in one year."

Some home improvements fall into a gray area as to their deductibility. For example, deducting the cost of painting the exterior of an owner-occupied home may be approved by some agents and denied by others, but such an improvement figures to get approval as a deduction on property that is rented out.

Since the profit derived when a property is sold is reduced by the cost of all commissions and expenses involved in selling, owners should be certain to retain all appropriate records. Of course, all (or capital) improvements should be added to the original cost of the house — provided the owner possesses the appropriate records — to reduce the capital gain. Expenses incurred to get the property ready for sale can also be added to the original cost, although the IRS generally limits these deductible expenses to those incurred within 90 days and paid for within 30 days of the sale.

According to IRS agent Lapin, the best advice regarding which records to keep can be summed up simply as, "When in doubt, keep the receipt."

The ultimate profitability in buying and selling real estate rests largely on reducing the share of the proceeds claimed by the IRS. Accurate records of all deductible expenses are the home investor's key to minimizing the tax liability and maximizing the profit in any transaction.

Glossary Of Real Estate Terms

A

Agent — A person who is licensed to sell real estate after passing the real estate sales examination. An agent is not a broker, the latter having passed a more demanding examination to obtain a broker's license.

Amenity — Some feature of a property that enhances its value. Amenities include community improvements that benefit all property within a given area.

Amortization — Reduction of a debt over a specified period of time, usually by installments.

Amortization Period — The length of time, typically measured in years, over which a loan is repaid.

Appraisal — An estimate of the value of property.

Appreciation — The increase in value of a piece of real estate.

Assessed Valuation — The taxing authority's estimate of the value of property for the purpose of imposing real estate taxes.

Assessment — The levy placed on a piece of property by a taxing authority. In a condominium or cooperative, the assessment also refers to the monthly charge each owner must pay to cover common expenses for operation and maintenance of the building.

Assessment Rolls — A public record indicating assessments against each property in a tax district.

Assignment — The transfer of a right or contract from one party to another.

Assumption — Agreement by a purchaser of property to take over the remaining mortgage or other liability of the seller.

B

Balloon (or Balloon Mortgage) — A loan in which a large part or all of the principal is due at a specified future date; until that date, the borrower pays just interest or interest plus a small part of the principal in regular installments.

Binder — A preliminary agreement between buyer and seller that includes the price, essential terms, and the signatures of both parties to the transaction.

Broker — A person who has passed a more demanding state examination than a real estate sales agent. Usually, the broker is either the principal in a real estate office or an associate who works for the principal broker.

Building Code — Local requirements that regulate housing design, materials, and construction to assure compliance with safety and health standards.

Buyer Profile — The characteristics (e.g., age, sex, marital status, family size, income, etc.) of a potential buyer of real estate.

Appendices

Buyer's Market — A real estate market in which the number of properties for sale is greater than the number of prospective buyers. A buyer's market typically results in lower prices for property.

C

Capital Gain Tax — The tax imposed by the federal government on the sale of property. Property held for more than a year receives favored tax status in that only half of the profit is subject to taxation, although a minimum tax is applicable to the other half in certain situations. (See example in "Profit By Selling").

Capital Improvement — A major addition or replacement to real estate that improves or extends the life of the property. The cost of a capital improvement can be added to the original cost of the property to reduce the net profit at the time of sale.

Closing — The final settlement between buyer and seller that includes the exchange of deed, financial arrangements, signing of notes, and disbursement of funds to parties involved in the transaction.

Closing Costs — The various expenses involved in completing a real estate transaction, including the cost of the title search, attorney's fees, mortgage fees, and prepaid items such as taxes and insurance.

Closing Statement — An estimate, required of mortgage lenders by the federal government, that covers the various expenses of closing. A copy of the statement is supposed to go to the borrower at least 12 days prior to closing.

Commission — The compensation paid to a real estate agent for selling a piece of property. The seller pays in most cases, and the amount is usually computed as a percentage (6 to 7 percent is most common) of the total sale price of the property.

Condominium — A form of property ownership in which the purchaser receives title to an individual unit in a multi-unit building and a proportionate share of ownership of common areas outside that unit. "Condominium" is used colloquially to mean the unit itself, i.e., the interior space of a non-rental apartment or townhouse.

Constant Payment — The equal monthly or annual payment on a mortgage over the life of the loan.

Contingency — A provision in a real estate contract for some problem or circumstance that, should it occur, will affect the transaction.

Contract Of Sale — An agreement signed by both buyer and seller to convey title to real estate after certain conditions have been met and payments made.

Contractor (or General Contractor) — A person or company who furnishes materials and labor for construction work at a specified price.

Contract Sale — An agreement in which the seller retains title to real estate until the buyer fully pays the agreed-upon price, usually over a specified term and in installments that include interest.

Conventional Loan — A loan from a private institution, such as a savings association, that does not include any government insurance against default.

Conversion — The change in a multi-unit building from rental to condominium ownership.

Cooperative — Ownership of multi-unit real estate in which participants hold stock in a corporation that actually owns the building. The corporation grants occupancy rights for units in the building to individual shareholders.

Custom-Built — A home that is individually designed and constructed, in contrast to homes built according to a pattern repeated throughout a subdivision.

D

Deed — A written document that legally conveys real estate ownership. A deed is transferred from one party to another when real estate is bought and sold.

Default — Failure to meet a mortgage commitment. Default may result in the surrender of property.

Deferred Tax — A tax liability that is not immediately due because government regulations postpone payment until a later date.

Deposit — A sum of money that binds the sale of real estate or assures payment of a larger sum at a later date. A deposit is frequently referred to as "earnest money."

Depreciation — A loss of value. Under federal tax laws, depreciation can be claimed even though no real loss occurs and the property does not actually deteriorate.

Detached House — A home that is located on its own lot and is not attached to any other building (unlike a townhouse).

Discount (or Discount Point) — The amount that the lender charges to make the loan, computed in terms of a percentage of the total amount borrowed.

Downpayment — The difference, payable in cash, between the sale price of real estate and the amount of the mortgage. A downpayment is nearly always required of the buyer to obtain the loan.

E

Earnest Money — See Deposit.

Empty Nester — A person or couple whose children have "left the nest," moving out to college or to their own residence.

Equity — The owner's interest in real estate, exclusive of mortgage debt.

Escrow — A fund in which buyers and sellers vest money to a third party for distribution at a later date according to the instructions of both parties. Costs for prorated taxes and insurance, deposits, title searches, and credit reports are maintained in an escrow account until needed.

Exclusive Listing — A written agreement between a seller and a real estate agent, providing the agent with the exclusive right to sell the property for a specified time. In some cases, the owner can retain the right to sell the property alone without payment of a commission.

Fair Market Rent — The amount of rent that a particular unit can command at a given time with no special considerations between tenant and landlord.

Fair Market Value — The amount that a knowledgeable buyer would pay a knowledgeable seller for a property after the property has been on the market for a sufficient time to test its selling power.

Federal Housing Administration — An agency of the federal government that (among other functions) insures loans, usually at a lower rate than private lending institutions. The FHA also sets standards of construction for property on which it offers loan insurance.

First Mortgage — The primary loan on the property, giving the holder of the mortgage first claim against the property in case of default.

Fixture — Property that becomes part of the real estate by being attached to it.

Foreclosure — A legal procedure initiated by the holder of a mortgage to take possession of property when the property owner fails to meet the payment obligations of the mortgage.

G

G.I. Loan — See Veterans Administration.

Gross Income — All income, as distinguished from net income, which is all income less expenses.

Guaranteed Loan — A loan guaranteed by the Veterans Administration or Federal Housing Administration, assuring the lender of repayment in the event of a borrower's default.

Guaranty — One party's promise to pay a debt or contracted obligation in event that the originally obligated party fails to do so. For example, the Veterans Administration's program of insuring home mortgages is called "loan guaranty."

H

Homeowners Association — An organization consisting of condominium owners who jointly control the operations and divide the expenses of community facilities and services.

Homeowners Policy — An insurance policy that protects individual owners against such perils as fire or wind damage, personal liability, and theft.

I

Improvement — Any change or addition to real estate, even ones that may not add to its value.

Income Property (or Income-Producing Property) — Real estate that returns a regular income to its owner. An apartment building is the most common form of income property.

Installment — The payment that a borrower makes on a loan, usually every month.

Insurable Value — The value of the property, less the value of the land and any other exclusions, to be insured.

Insured Loan — A loan in which the lender is guaranteed repayment either by a private mortgage insurance company or by a federal agency.

Interest — Payment for the use of money.

Interest Rate — A percentage of a loan charged as payment for the use of the money. The interest rate is usually expressed as the percentage per annum.

Interim Financing — A short-term loan that covers a borrower's financial needs of brief duration, such as the time between the sale of one property and the purchase of another.

J

Joint Tenancy — Equal ownership of property by two or more persons, providing for the survivor(s) taking over the share of any deceased party or parties to the agreement.

Junior Mortgage — A claim that is secondary to the primary loan on the property. A second mortgage is one common type of junior mortgage.

L

Land Trust — A device in which the owner places title to the property with another party, usually a financial institution, while retaining the benefits of ownership. The land trust is frequently used to conceal property ownership and to keep the property out of probate (though it is still taxable).

Lease — A written agreement containing the conditions for possession of property for a stated period of time and for a specific consideration.

Level Payment Mortgage — See Constant Payment.

Leverage — The technique of using borrowed money to increase the return on an investment. For example, a loan in which the borrower has had to make no downpayment is 100 percent leveraged.

Listing — A written authorization to sell or lease property.

MAI — Member of the Appraisal Institute, an appraiser who usually does not handle home appraisals unless employed by a savings and loan association.

Market Rent — See Fair Market Rent.

Market Value — See Fair Market Value.

Master Plan — The document that a community develops to control its residential, industrial, and commercial growth. The master plan also designates areas where recreational and community facilities will be located.

Maturity — The date when a mortgage becomes due and payable.

Mechanical System — The heating, air conditioning, plumbing, and venting systems of a home.

Minimum Property Standard — Regulations of the Federal Housing Administration governing the minimum acceptable standards in construction and materials for homes insured by that agency and by the Veterans Administration.

Mortgage — A loan in which real estate serves as the security.

Mortgage Insurance — A guarantee to the lender that the mortgage will be paid off in event of the borrower's default or death.

Mortgage Insurance Premium — A sum paid, usually on a monthly basis, to obtain mortgage insurance from a government agency or private insurer. Typically, the premium amounts to one-quarter to one-half of one percent of the balance due on the mortgage.

Multiple Listing — An agreement between a seller and an individual broker that property will be listed by all brokers cooperating in a multiple listing service.

Net Income — The difference between gross income and expenses.

Net Spendable — The actual cash left over from gross income after deducting operating expenses, principal and interest payments, and taxes.

Office Park — A campus-like grouping of several office buildings of moderate size scattered across a large landscaped area.

Open-End Mortgage — A mortgage that permits the borrower to increase the outstanding loan, with the approval of the lender, by adding back the accumulated equity and a percentage of the value appreciation.

Operating Expenses — All the expenses of owning a property, excluding real estate taxes, interest, depreciation, and mortgage amortization.

Option — Agreement for the sale of property within a given period of time at a specified price.

P

PITI — Abbreviation for Principal, Interest, Taxes, and Insurance.

Planned Unit Development — Abbreviated PUD, refers to a comprehensive plan for development of an area. The plan, which usually requires community government approval, includes all the schools, recreational facilities, commercial, and employment centers in the area.

Point — One percent of the principal amount of the loan. The lender frequently charges the borrower one or more points at the time of closing as the cost of making the loan.

Prepayment — Advance payments on a mortgage that reduce the outstanding loan prior to maturity. The mortgage usually stipulates whether prepayment is permitted and in what amount; in some cases, lenders charge a penalty for prepayment.

Principal (or Principal Balance) — The amount yet to be paid on the total sum borrowed.

Private Mortgage Insurance — A plan to insure the mortgage above the level that a lender will approve, resulting in lower downpayment requirements for the borrower. Private mortgage insurance, usually carrying a fee of one-quarter to one-half of one percent of the outstanding loan, can enable a borrower to put as little as 5 percent down on the purchase of a property.

Probate — The legal settlement of an estate upon an individual's death.

Prorate — The allocation of shares of an obligation between two or more parties, usually between buyer and seller.

R

Realtor — A broker or the sales associate of a broker who holds membership in the National Association of Realtors and agrees to abide by that organization's standards of conduct.

Refinancing — The process of paying off one loan by taking out another loan, using the same real estate as security.

Rehabilitation — Upgrading or modernizing property to restore it to good use and maximum value.

Replacement Cost — The amount needed to restore materials that have been damaged or lost to the condition they were in at the time of the damage or loss.

Reproduction Cost — The money needed to reproduce a building, less an allowance for depreciation.

Rowhouse — See Townhouse.

S

Sales Contract — See Contract Of Sale.

Savings And Loan Association — An association of savers which makes loans primarily to borrowers seeking home mortgages. Savings and loan associations are chartered and regulated by either the federal or state government.

Secondary Financing — Financing of real estate by a party whose claim comes second to the holder of the first mortgage.

Second Mortgage — An additional loan beyond the first mortgage with second priority in case of default.

Seller's Market — A real estate market in which the number of buyers is greater than the number of properties for sale. A seller's market typically results in higher prices for property.

Appendices

Septic System — A sewage disposal process in which an individual tank is located on the property to decompose and distribute waste material.

Settlement — See Closing.

Speculative Construction — Construction of a home without a prior sales agreement.

SRA — Abbreviation for Senior Residential Appraiser of the Society of Real Estate Appraisers, usually a specialist in appraising homes.

Subcontractor — A skilled tradesman, such as a plumber or electrician, who performs construction work for individuals or general contractors.

Subdivision — Land that has been divided into a number of parcels for immediate or future sale.

Term Mortgage — A loan over a specified length of time, usually not more than five years, during which the borrower only makes interest payments. The principal is due at the end of the term.

Tight Money — A situation in which lending institutions do not receive the normal flow of savings and consequently restrict loans to established customers and raise interest rates.

Title Insurance — A contract which assures that an owner will not suffer any loss (such as unrevealed liens against the property or claims to ownership by parties other than the seller) due to defects in the title.

Title Search — The process by which a title company examines records to determine the facts of property ownership.

Townhouse — A housing unit that shares one or more walls in common with adjoining housing units, usually with a similar exterior configuration. The owner may or may not share expenses for maintaining the area outside the building and may or may not own the adjacent yard.

Trust — See Land Trust.

Usury — A rate of interest greater than the legal rate.

Variable Rate Mortgage — A loan that allows for adjustment of the interest rate according to the going rate at specified times. Popular in California and gaining ground nationally, the variable rate mortgage is reviewed periodically and the rate moved up or down according to the current loan market.

Veterans Administration — A federal agency that (among other functions) guarantees loans against default for honorably discharged members of the military services. Loans with a VA guaranty typically provide for a lower down-payment and a lower-than-market interest rate.

Wraparound Mortgage — A loan that covers the debt on an existing mortgage and advances an additional amount based on the property's appreciation. The borrower makes payments to the lender of the wraparound mortgage, who then makes payments on the first mortgage.

Yield — The return on investment, usually expressed as an annual rate.

Zoning — The use to which a property may be put as specified by community or county authorities.

Appendices

Principal And Interest Tables

AMORTIZATION refers to payment of a debt through installments, usually equal monthly sums. Although the installments remain equal, the interest payments decline with each passing year and the principal payments increase until the mortgage is paid off.

Since most of the home mortgages over the last few years have been negotiated with an interest rate in the range of 7 to 10 percent and a repayment period of 20, 25, or 30 years, the following tables should help both present and prospective homeowners in computing which financing arrangements are most advantageous.

The tables show how much interest and principal a homeowner pays annually during the life of 20-, 25-, and 30-year loans. The figures shown refer to amounts per $1,000. Thus, for example, in the first year of a 7 percent loan to be repaid over 25 years, the owner will pay $69.51 in interest and $15.33 in principal per $1,000 of the mortgage. The remaining balance after one payment will be $984.67 per $1,000. To compute how much this would amount to on a $30,000 mortgage, one would merely multiply each number by 30; the result would be a first-year payment of $2,085.30 in interest and $459.90 in principal. The remaining balance on the loan would be $29,540.10.

Amortization tables can be especially useful to homeowners deciding whether to refinance. The investor involved in refinancing generally trades a low-interest loan for a mortgage carrying substantially higher interest payments. Just how high these new payments will be can be computed on the following tables.

20 Year Term

7% Interest

$7.76 monthly payment

Year	Interest	Principal	Balance
1	69.24	23.88	976.12
2	67.52	25.60	950.52
3	65.67	27.45	923.07
4	63.68	29.44	893.63
5	61.54	31.58	862.05
6	59.28	33.84	828.21
7	56.83	36.29	791.92
8	54.19	38.93	752.99
9	51.37	41.75	711.24
10	48.38	44.74	666.50
11	45.12	48.00	618.50
12	41.67	51.45	567.05
13	37.95	55.17	511.88
14	33.97	59.15	452.73
15	29.68	63.44	389.29
16	25.10	68.02	321.27
17	20.19	72.93	248.34
18	14.90	78.22	170.12
19	9.25	83.87	86.25
20	3.19	86.25	0

7¼% Interest

$7.91 monthly payment

Year	Interest	Principal	Balance
1	71.74	23.18	976.82
2	70.01	24.91	951.91
3	68.13	26.79	925.12
4	66.13	28.79	896.33
5	63.96	30.96	865.37
6	61.65	33.27	832.10
7	59.16	35.76	796.34
8	56.47	38.45	757.89
9	53.61	41.31	716.58
10	50.50	44.42	672.16
11	47.17	47.75	624.41
12	43.59	51.33	573.08
13	39.74	55.18	517.90
14	35.58	59.34	458.56
15	31.16	63.76	394.80
16	26.37	68.55	326.25
17	21.25	73.67	252.58
18	15.72	79.20	173.38
19	9.79	85.13	88.25
20	3.40	88.25	0

20 Year Term

7½% Interest

$8.06 monthly payment

Year	Interest	Principal	Balance
1	74.24	22.48	977.52
2	72.49	24.23	953.29
3	70.63	26.09	927.20
4	68.58	28.14	899.06
5	66.40	30.32	868.74
6	64.04	32.68	836.06
7	61.51	35.21	800.85
8	58.81	37.91	762.94
9	55.83	40.89	722.05
10	52.66	44.06	677.99
11	49.25	47.47	630.52
12	45.56	51.16	579.36
13	41.58	55.14	524.22
14	37.32	59.40	464.82
15	32.69	64.03	400.79
16	27.73	68.99	331.80
17	22.37	74.35	257.45
18	16.61	80.11	177.34
19	10.37	86.35	90.99
20	3.67	90.99	0

7¾% Interest

$8.21 monthly payment

Year	Interest	Principal	Balance
1	76.74	21.78	978.22
2	75.00	23.52	954.70
3	73.10	25.42	929.28
4	71.05	27.47	901.81
5	68.84	29.68	872.13
6	66.47	32.05	840.08
7	63.89	34.63	805.45
8	61.09	37.43	768.02
9	58.11	40.41	727.61
10	54.86	43.66	683.95
11	51.35	47.17	636.78
12	47.56	50.96	585.82
13	43.49	55.03	530.79
14	39.05	59.47	471.32
15	34.28	64.24	407.08
16	29.12	69.40	337.68
17	23.52	75.00	262.68
18	17.53	80.99	181.69
19	11.01	87.51	94.18
20	3.99	94.18	0

20
Year Term

8% Interest

$8.37 monthly payment

Year	Interest	Principal	Balance
1	79.24	21.20	978.80
2	77.47	22.97	955.83
3	75.58	24.86	930.97
4	73.49	26.95	904.02
5	71.29	29.15	874.87
6	68.85	31.59	843.28
7	66.21	34.23	809.05
8	63.37	37.07	771.98
9	60.32	40.12	731.86
10	56.99	43.45	688.41
11	53.36	47.08	641.33
12	49.46	50.98	590.35
13	45.26	55.18	535.17
14	40.67	59.77	475.40
15	35.67	64.77	410.63
16	30.31	70.13	340.50
17	24.51	75.93	264.57
18	18.20	82.24	182.33
19	11.33	89.11	93.22
20	3.97	93.22	0

8¼% Interest

$8.52 monthly payment

Year	Interest	Principal	Balance
1	81.74	20.51	979.50
2	79.98	22.27	957.24
3	78.08	24.17	933.07
4	76.01	26.24	906.83
5	73.76	28.49	878.34
6	71.32	30.93	847.42
7	68.67	33.58	813.84
8	65.79	36.46	777.38
9	62.66	39.59	737.80
10	59.27	42.98	694.83
11	55.59	46.66	648.17
12	51.59	50.66	597.52
13	47.25	55.00	542.52
14	42.54	59.71	482.82
15	37.42	64.83	417.99
16	31.87	70.38	347.62
17	25.84	76.41	271.21
18	19.29	82.96	188.25
19	12.18	90.07	98.19
20	4.46	97.79	.40

20
Year Term

8½% Interest

$8.68 monthly payment

Year	Interest	Principal	Balance
1	84.24	19.93	980.08
2	82.48	21.69	958.40
3	80.56	23.61	934.79
4	78.48	25.69	909.10
5	76.21	27.96	881.15
6	73.73	30.44	850.71
7	71.04	33.13	817.59
8	68.12	36.05	781.55
9	64.93	39.24	742.31
10	61.46	42.71	699.61
11	57.69	46.48	653.13
12	53.58	50.59	602.55
13	49.11	55.06	547.49
14	44.24	59.93	487.57
15	38.95	65.22	422.35
16	33.18	70.99	351.37
17	26.91	77.26	274.11
18	20.08	84.09	190.02
19	12.65	91.52	98.51
20	4.56	99.61	1.10

8¾% Interest

$8.84 monthly payment

Year	Interest	Principal	Balance
1	86.74	19.35	980.66
2	84.98	21.11	959.56
3	83.06	23.03	936.53
4	80.96	25.13	911.40
5	78.67	27.42	883.99
6	76.17	29.92	854.07
7	73.45	32.64	821.44
8	70.47	35.62	785.83
9	67.23	38.86	746.97
10	63.69	42.40	704.58
11	59.83	46.26	658.32
12	55.62	50.47	607.85
13	51.02	55.07	552.79
14	46.00	60.09	492.70
15	40.53	65.56	427.15
16	34.56	71.53	355.62
17	28.04	78.05	277.57
18	20.93	85.16	192.42
19	13.17	92.92	99.51
20	4.71	101.38	1.87

20
Year Term

9% Interest

$9.00 monthly payment

Year	Interest	Principal	Balance
1	89.24	18.76	981.24
2	87.47	20.53	960.71
3	85.56	22.44	938.27
4	83.45	24.55	913.72
5	81.14	26.86	886.86
6	78.64	29.36	857.50
7	75.83	32.17	825.33
8	72.85	35.15	790.18
9	69.56	38.44	751.74
10	65.96	42.04	709.70
11	62.01	45.99	663.71
12	57.70	50.30	613.41
13	52.97	55.03	558.38
14	47.80	60.20	498.18
15	42.19	65.81	432.37
16	35.99	72.01	360.36
17	29.20	78.80	281.56
18	21.86	86.14	195.42
19	13.76	94.24	101.18
20	4.93	101.18	0

20
Year Term

 **Interest**   9½% **Interest**

$9.16 monthly payment   **$9.32 monthly payment**

Year	Interest	Principal	Balance	Year	Interest	Principal	Balance
1	91.75	18.18	981.83	1	94.25	17.60	982.41
2	89.99	19.94	961.89	2	92.51	19.34	963.01
3	88.07	21.86	940.04	3	90.59	21.26	941.81
4	85.96	23.97	916.07	4	88.48	23.37	918.45
5	83.65	26.28	889.79	5	86.16	25.69	892.76
6	81.11	28.82	860.98	6	83.61	28.24	864.52
7	78.33	31.60	829.38	7	80.81	31.04	833.48
8	75.28	34.65	794.73	8	77.73	34.12	799.36
9	71.93	38.00	756.74	9	74.34	37.51	761.86
10	68.27	41.66	715.08	10	70.62	41.23	720.63
11	64.25	45.68	669.40	11	66.52	45.33	675.31
12	59.84	50.09	619.31	12	62.03	49.82	625.49
13	55.00	54.93	564.39	13	57.08	54.77	570.73
14	49.70	60.23	504.16	14	51.65	60.20	510.53
15	43.89	66.04	438.13	15	45.67	66.18	444.36
16	37.51	72.42	365.71	16	39.11	72.74	371.62
17	30.52	79.41	286.31	17	31.89	79.96	291.66
18	22.86	87.07	199.24	18	23.95	87.90	203.76
19	14.45	95.48	103.77	19	15.23	96.62	107.15
20	5.24	104.69	0.91	20	5.64	106.21	0.94

20
Year Term

9¾% Interest

$9.49 monthly payment

Year	Interest	Principal	Balance
1	96.75	17.14	982.87
2	95.01	18.88	963.99
3	93.08	20.81	943.19
4	90.96	22.93	920.26
5	88.62	25.27	895.00
6	86.04	27.85	867.16
7	83.21	30.68	836.48
8	80.08	33.81	802.67
9	76.63	37.26	765.42
10	72.83	41.06	724.36
11	68.64	45.25	679.12
12	64.03	49.86	629.26
13	58.95	54.94	574.32
14	53.34	60.55	513.78
15	47.17	66.72	447.07
16	40.37	73.52	373.55
17	32.87	81.02	292.53
18	24.61	89.28	203.25
19	15.50	98.39	104.87
20	5.47	108.42	3.55

10% Interest

$9.66 monthly payment

Year	Interest	Principal	Balance
1	99.25	16.67	983.33
2	97.49	18.43	964.90
3	95.59	20.33	944.57
4	93.44	22.48	922.09
5	91.09	24.83	897.26
6	88.51	27.41	869.85
7	85.62	30.30	839.55
8	82.45	33.47	806.08
9	78.94	36.98	769.10
10	75.08	40.84	728.26
11	70.81	45.11	683.15
12	66.07	49.85	633.30
13	60.86	55.06	578.24
14	55.11	60.81	517.43
15	48.71	67.21	450.22
16	41.68	74.24	375.98
17	33.90	82.02	293.96
18	25.32	90.60	203.36
19	15.83	100.09	103.27
20	5.35	103.27	0

25 Year Term

7% Interest

$7.07 monthly payment

Year	Interest	Principal	Balance
1	69.51	15.33	984.67
2	68.40	16.44	968.23
3	67.20	17.64	950.59
4	65.94	18.90	931.69
5	64.62	20.22	911.47
6	63.12	21.72	889.75
7	61.55	23.29	866.46
8	59.85	24.99	841.47
9	58.06	26.78	814.69
10	56.12	28.72	785.97
11	54.05	30.79	755.18
12	51.81	33.03	722.15
13	49.44	35.40	686.75
14	46.87	37.97	648.78
15	44.14	40.70	608.08
16	41.20	43.64	564.44
17	38.03	46.81	517.63
18	34.65	50.19	467.44
19	31.02	53.82	413.62
20	27.12	57.72	355.90
21	22.99	61.85	294.05
22	18.48	66.36	227.69
23	13.67	71.17	156.52
24	8.52	76.32	80.20
25	3.01	80.20	0

7¼% Interest

$7.23 monthly payment

Year	Interest	Principal	Balance
1	72.02	14.74	985.26
2	70.91	15.85	969.41
3	69.72	17.04	952.37
4	68.44	18.32	934.05
5	67.01	19.75	914.30
6	65.58	21.18	893.12
7	64.01	22.75	870.37
8	62.30	24.46	845.91
9	60.47	26.29	819.62
10	58.49	28.27	791.35
11	56.39	30.37	760.98
12	54.10	32.66	728.32
13	51.66	35.10	693.22
14	49.02	37.74	655.48
15	46.20	40.56	614.92
16	43.15	43.61	571.31
17	39.89	46.87	524.44
18	36.35	50.41	474.03
19	32.59	54.17	419.86
20	28.53	58.23	361.63
21	24.15	62.61	299.02
22	19.47	67.29	231.73
23	14.43	72.33	159.40
24	8.98	77.78	81.62
25	3.17	81.62	0

25 Year Term

7½% Interest

$7.39 monthly payment

Year	Interest	Principal	Balance
1	74.52	14.16	985.84
2	73.42	15.26	970.58
3	72.23	16.45	954.13
4	70.96	17.72	936.41
5	69.54	19.14	917.27
6	68.11	20.57	896.70
7	66.48	22.20	874.50
8	64.77	23.91	850.59
9	62.92	25.76	824.83
10	60.93	27.75	797.08
11	58.78	29.90	767.18
12	56.44	32.24	734.94
13	53.94	34.74	700.20
14	51.23	37.45	662.75
15	48.33	40.35	622.40
16	45.21	43.47	578.98
17	41.83	46.85	532.08
18	38.20	50.48	481.60
19	34.28	54.40	427.20
20	30.05	58.63	368.57
21	25.51	63.17	305.40
22	20.59	68.09	237.31
23	15.30	73.38	163.93
24	9.59	79.09	84.84
25	3.47	84.84	0

7¾% Interest

$7.56 monthly payment

Year	Interest	Principal	Balance
1	77.02	13.70	986.30
2	75.92	14.80	971.50
3	74.72	16.00	956.50
4	73.45	17.27	938.23
5	72.06	18.66	919.57
6	70.57	20.15	899.42
7	68.95	21.77	877.65
8	67.19	23.53	854.12
9	65.30	25.42	828.70
10	63.28	27.44	801.26
11	61.05	29.67	771.59
12	58.67	32.05	739.54
13	56.10	34.62	704.92
14	53.29	37.43	667.49
15	50.31	40.41	627.08
16	47.06	43.66	583.42
17	43.57	47.15	536.27
18	39.77	50.95	485.32
19	35.69	55.03	430.29
20	31.26	59.46	370.83
21	26.51	64.21	306.62
22	21.33	69.39	237.23
23	15.72	75.00	162.23
24	9.74	80.98	81.25
25	3.22	81.25	0

25 Year Term

8% Interest

$7.72 monthly payment

Year	Interest	Principal	Balance
1	79.53	13.11	986.89
2	78.43	14.21	972.68
3	77.26	15.38	957.30
4	75.99	16.65	940.65
5	74.58	18.06	922.59
6	73.10	19.54	903.05
7	71.49	21.15	881.90
8	69.72	22.92	858.98
9	67.83	24.81	834.17
10	65.76	26.88	807.29
11	63.52	29.12	778.17
12	61.11	31.53	746.64
13	58.50	34.14	712.50
14	55.67	36.97	675.53
15	52.59	40.05	635.48
16	49.26	43.38	592.10
17	45.68	46.96	545.14
18	41.76	50.88	494.26
19	37.57	55.07	439.19
20	32.98	59.66	379.53
21	28.03	64.61	314.92
22	22.65	69.99	244.93
23	16.85	75.79	169.14
24	10.53	82.11	87.03
25	3.74	87.03	0

8¼% Interest

$7.88 monthly payment

Year	Interest	Principal	Balance
1	82.04	12.53	987.48
2	80.96	13.61	973.88
3	79.80	14.77	959.11
4	78.53	16.04	943.08
5	77.16	17.41	925.68
6	75.67	18.90	906.78
7	74.05	20.52	886.27
8	72.29	22.28	863.99
9	70.38	24.19	839.81
10	68.31	26.26	813.56
11	66.06	28.51	785.05
12	63.62	30.95	754.11
13	60.97	33.60	720.51
14	58.09	36.48	684.03
15	54.96	39.61	644.43
16	51.57	43.00	601.43
17	47.88	46.69	554.75
18	43.88	50.69	504.07
19	39.54	55.03	449.05
20	34.83	59.74	389.31
21	29.71	64.86	324.45
22	24.15	70.42	254.03
23	18.11	76.46	177.58
24	11.56	83.01	94.58
25	4.45	90.12	4.46

25 Year Term

8½% Interest

$8.05 monthly payment

Year	Interest	Principal	Balance
1	84.54	12.07	987.94
2	83.48	13.13	974.81
3	82.32	14.29	960.52
4	81.05	15.56	944.97
5	79.68	16.93	928.04
6	78.18	18.43	909.62
7	76.55	20.06	889.57
8	74.78	21.83	867.74
9	72.85	23.76	843.99
10	70.75	25.86	818.14
11	68.47	28.14	790.00
12	65.98	30.63	759.37
13	63.27	33.34	726.04
14	60.33	36.28	689.76
15	57.12	39.49	650.28
16	53.63	42.98	607.30
17	49.83	46.78	560.53
18	45.70	50.91	509.62
19	41.20	55.41	454.21
20	36.30	60.31	393.91
21	30.97	65.64	328.27
22	25.17	71.44	256.83
23	18.85	77.76	179.08
24	11.98	84.63	94.45
25	4.50	92.11	2.35

8¾% Interest

$8.22 monthly payment

Year	Interest	Principal	Balance
1	87.05	11.60	988.41
2	85.99	12.66	975.75
3	84.84	13.81	961.95
4	83.58	15.07	946.88
5	82.21	16.44	930.44
6	80.71	17.94	912.51
7	79.08	19.57	892.94
8	77.29	21.36	871.59
9	75.35	23.30	848.29
10	73.23	25.42	822.88
11	70.91	27.74	795.14
12	68.39	30.26	764.88
13	65.63	33.02	731.87
14	62.62	36.03	695.84
15	59.34	39.31	656.54
16	55.76	42.89	613.65
17	51.85	46.80	566.86
18	47.59	51.06	515.80
19	42.94	55.71	460.09
20	37.86	60.79	399.31
21	32.33	66.32	332.99
22	26.29	72.36	260.64
23	19.69	78.96	181.68
24	12.50	86.15	95.54
25	4.65	94.00	1.55

25 Year Term

9% Interest

$8.40 monthly payment

Year	Interest	Principal	Balance
1	89.54	11.26	988.74
2	88.49	12.31	976.43
3	87.34	13.46	962.97
4	86.07	14.73	948.24
5	84.66	16.14	932.10
6	83.18	17.62	914.48
7	81.52	19.28	895.20
8	79.72	21.08	874.12
9	77.73	23.07	851.05
10	75.58	25.22	825.83
11	74.10	27.60	798.23
12	70.62	30.18	768.05
13	67.79	33.01	735.04
14	64.69	36.11	698.93
15	61.29	39.51	659.42
16	57.60	43.20	616.22
17	53.56	47.24	568.98
18	49.12	51.68	517.30
19	44.27	56.53	460.77
20	38.96	61.84	398.93
21	33.17	67.63	331.30
22	26.81	73.99	257.31
23	19.86	80.94	176.37
24	12.27	88.53	87.84
25	3.96	87.84	0

9¼% Interest

$8.56 monthly payment

Year	Interest	Principal	Balance
1	92.06	10.67	989.34
2	91.03	11.70	977.65
3	89.90	12.83	964.82
4	88.66	14.07	950.76
5	87.31	15.42	935.35
6	85.82	16.91	918.44
7	84.19	18.54	899.90
8	82.40	20.33	879.58
9	80.44	22.29	857.29
10	78.28	24.45	832.85
11	75.93	26.80	806.05
12	73.34	29.39	776.66
13	70.50	32.23	744.44
14	67.39	35.34	709.10
15	63.98	38.75	670.36
16	60.24	42.49	627.88
17	56.14	46.59	581.29
18	51.64	51.09	530.21
19	46.71	56.02	474.20
20	41.31	61.42	412.78
21	35.38	67.35	345.44
22	28.88	73.85	271.59
23	21.75	80.98	190.62
24	13.94	88.79	101.83
25	5.36	97.37	4.47

25 Year Term

9½% Interest

$8.74 monthly payment

Year	Interest	Principal	Balance
1	94.56	10.33	989.68
2	93.54	11.35	978.34
3	92.41	12.48	965.86
4	91.17	13.72	952.15
5	89.81	15.08	937.08
6	88.32	16.57	920.52
7	86.67	18.22	902.31
8	84.87	20.02	882.29
9	82.88	22.01	860.28
10	80.70	24.19	836.10
11	78.30	26.59	809.51
12	75.66	29.23	780.28
13	72.76	32.13	748.15
14	69.57	35.32	712.83
15	66.06	38.83	674.01
16	62.21	42.68	631.33
17	57.97	46.92	584.42
18	53.32	51.57	532.85
19	48.20	56.69	476.17
20	42.57	62.32	413.85
21	36.39	68.50	345.36
22	29.59	75.30	270.07
23	22.12	82.77	187.30
24	13.90	90.99	96.32
25	4.87	100.02	3.69

9¾% Interest

$8.91 monthly payment

Year	Interest	Principal	Balance
1	97.07	9.86	990.15
2	96.07	10.86	979.30
3	94.96	11.97	967.33
4	93.74	13.19	954.15
5	92.40	14.53	939.62
6	90.91	16.02	923.61
7	89.28	17.65	905.96
8	87.48	19.45	886.52
9	85.50	21.43	865.09
10	83.31	23.62	841.48
11	80.91	26.02	815.47
12	78.25	28.68	786.79
13	75.33	31.60	755.20
14	72.11	34.82	720.38
15	68.56	38.37	682.01
16	64.64	42.29	639.73
17	60.33	46.60	593.14
18	55.58	51.35	541.80
19	50.35	56.58	485.22
20	44.58	62.35	422.87
21	38.22	68.71	354.16
22	31.21	75.72	278.45
23	23.49	83.44	195.02
24	14.98	91.95	103.07
25	5.61	101.32	1.75

25
Year Term

10% Interest

Year	Interest	Principal	Balance
\$9.09 monthly payment			
1	99.56	9.52	990.48
2	98.57	10.51	979.97
3	97.48	11.60	968.37
4	96.25	12.83	955.54
5	94.93	14.15	941.39
6	93.44	15.64	925.75
7	91.78	17.30	908.45
8	90.01	19.07	889.38
9	87.99	21.09	868.29
10	85.78	23.30	844.99
11	83.33	25.75	819.24
12	80.63	28.45	790.79
13	77.68	31.40	759.39
14	74.39	34.69	724.70
15	70.74	38.34	686.36
16	66.74	42.34	644.02
17	62.29	46.79	597.23
18	57.39	51.69	545.54
19	51.96	57.12	488.42
20	46.01	63.07	425.35
21	39.37	69.71	355.64
22	32.09	76.99	278.65
23	24.06	85.02	193.63
24	15.13	93.95	99.68
25	5.29	99.68	0

30 Year Term

7% Interest

$6.65 monthly payment

Year	Interest	Principal	Balance
1	69.68	10.13	989.88
2	68.95	10.86	979.03
3	68.17	11.64	967.40
4	67.33	12.48	954.92
5	66.43	13.38	941.54
6	65.46	14.35	927.19
7	64.42	15.39	911.81
8	63.31	16.50	895.31
9	62.12	17.69	877.62
10	60.84	18.97	858.65
11	59.47	20.34	838.31
12	58.00	21.81	816.50
13	56.42	23.39	793.12
14	54.73	25.08	768.04
15	52.92	26.89	741.15
16	50.97	28.84	712.32
17	48.89	30.92	681.40
18	46.65	33.16	648.25
19	44.26	35.55	612.70
20	41.69	38.12	574.58
21	38.93	40.88	533.71
22	35.98	43.83	489.88
23	32.81	47.00	442.88
24	29.41	50.40	392.48
25	25.77	54.04	338.45
26	21.86	57.95	280.50
27	17.67	62.14	218.37
28	13.18	66.63	151.74
29	8.36	71.45	80.30
30	3.20	76.61	3.70

7¼% Interest

$6.82 monthly payment

Year	Interest	Principal	Balance
1	72.19	9.66	990.35
2	71.46	10.39	979.97
3	70.69	11.16	968.81
4	69.85	12.00	956.81
5	68.95	12.90	943.92
6	67.98	13.87	930.06
7	66.95	14.90	915.16
8	65.83	16.02	899.14
9	64.63	17.22	881.93
10	63.34	18.51	863.42
11	61.95	19.90	843.52
12	60.46	21.39	822.14
13	58.86	22.99	799.15
14	57.13	24.72	774.43
15	55.28	26.57	747.87
16	53.29	28.56	719.31
17	51.15	30.70	688.62
18	48.85	33.00	655.62
19	46.37	35.48	620.15
20	43.71	38.14	582.02
21	40.86	40.99	541.03
22	37.78	44.07	496.97
23	34.48	47.37	449.60
24	30.93	50.92	398.69
25	27.11	54.74	343.96
26	23.01	58.84	285.13
27	18.60	63.25	221.88
28	13.86	67.99	153.90
29	8.77	73.08	80.82
30	3.29	78.56	2.26

30 Year Term

7½% Interest

$6.99 monthly payment

Year	Interest	Principal	Balance
1	74.69	9.20	990.81
2	73.98	9.91	980.91
3	73.21	10.68	970.23
4	72.38	11.51	958.73
5	71.49	12.40	946.33
6	70.53	13.36	932.98
7	69.49	14.40	918.58
8	68.37	15.52	903.07
9	67.17	16.72	886.35
10	65.87	18.02	868.34
11	64.47	19.42	848.92
12	62.96	20.93	828.00
13	61.34	22.55	805.46
14	59.59	24.30	781.16
15	57.70	26.19	754.98
16	55.67	28.22	726.77
17	53.48	30.41	696.36
18	51.12	32.77	663.60
19	48.58	35.31	628.29
20	45.84	38.05	590.24
21	42.88	41.01	549.24
22	39.70	44.19	505.06
23	36.27	47.62	457.44
24	32.57	51.32	406.13
25	28.59	55.30	350.83
26	24.30	59.59	291.24
27	19.67	64.22	227.03
28	14.69	69.20	157.83
29	9.31	74.58	83.26
30	3.52	80.37	2.90

7¾% Interest

$7.16 monthly payment

Year	Interest	Principal	Balance
1	77.20	8.73	991.28
2	76.50	9.43	981.85
3	75.74	10.19	971.67
4	74.92	11.01	960.67
5	74.04	11.89	948.78
6	73.09	12.84	935.94
7	72.05	13.88	922.07
8	70.94	14.99	907.09
9	69.74	16.19	890.90
10	68.44	17.49	873.41
11	67.03	18.90	854.52
12	65.52	20.41	834.11
13	63.88	22.05	812.06
14	62.11	23.82	788.24
15	60.19	25.74	762.51
16	58.13	27.80	734.71
17	55.89	30.04	704.68
18	53.48	32.45	672.23
19	50.87	35.06	637.18
20	48.06	37.87	599.32
21	45.02	40.91	558.41
22	41.73	44.20	514.22
23	38.18	47.75	466.48
24	34.35	51.58	414.90
25	30.21	55.72	359.19
26	25.73	60.20	299.00
27	20.90	65.03	233.97
28	15.68	70.25	163.72
29	10.03	75.90	87.83
30	3.94	81.99	5.85

Appendices

30 Year Term

8% Interest

$7.34 monthly payment

Year	Interest	Principal	Balance
1	79.70	8.39	991.62
2	79.01	9.08	982.54
3	78.25	9.84	972.71
4	77.44	10.65	962.06
5	76.55	11.54	950.53
6	75.60	12.49	938.04
7	74.56	13.53	924.52
8	73.44	14.65	909.87
9	72.22	15.87	894.00
10	70.90	17.19	876.82
11	69.48	18.61	858.21
12	67.93	20.16	838.06
13	66.26	21.83	816.24
14	64.45	23.64	792.60
15	62.49	25.60	767.01
16	60.36	27.73	739.28
17	58.06	30.03	709.26
18	55.57	32.52	676.75
19	52.87	35.22	641.53
20	49.95	38.14	603.40
21	46.78	41.31	562.10
22	43.36	44.73	517.37
23	39.64	48.45	468.93
24	35.62	52.47	416.46
25	31.27	56.82	359.65
26	26.55	61.54	298.11
27	21.45	66.64	231.48
28	15.91	72.18	159.30
29	9.92	78.17	81.14
30	3.44	84.65	3.50

8¼% Interest

$7.51 monthly payment

Year	Interest	Principal	Balance
1	82.21	7.92	992.09
2	81.53	8.60	983.50
3	80.80	9.33	974.17
4	80.00	10.13	964.04
5	79.13	11.00	953.04
6	78.19	11.94	941.10
7	77.16	12.97	928.14
8	76.05	14.08	914.07
9	74.85	15.28	898.79
10	73.54	16.59	882.20
11	72.12	18.01	864.19
12	70.57	19.56	844.64
13	68.90	21.23	823.41
14	67.08	23.05	800.36
15	65.10	25.03	775.34
16	62.96	27.17	748.17
17	60.63	29.50	718.68
18	58.10	32.03	686.65
19	55.36	34.77	651.89
20	52.38	37.75	614.14
21	49.14	40.99	573.16
22	45.63	44.50	528.67
23	41.82	48.31	480.36
24	37.68	52.45	427.92
25	33.19	56.94	370.98
26	28.31	61.82	309.16
27	23.01	67.12	242.05
28	17.26	72.87	169.18
29	11.02	79.11	90.07
30	4.24	85.89	4.19

30

Year Term

8½% Interest

$7.69 monthly payment

Year	Interest	Principal	Balance
1	84.71	7.58	922.43
2	84.05	8.24	984.20
3	83.32	8.97	975.23
4	82.52	9.77	965.47
5	81.66	10.63	954.84
6	80.72	11.57	943.28
7	79.70	12.59	930.70
8	78.59	13.70	917.00
9	77.38	14.91	902.09
10	76.06	16.23	885.87
11	74.63	17.66	868.21
12	73.06	19.23	848.99
13	71.37	20.92	828.07
14	69.52	22.77	805.30
15	67.50	24.79	780.52
16	65.31	26.98	753.55
17	62.93	29.36	724.20
18	60.34	31.95	692.25
19	57.51	34.78	657.47
20	54.44	37.85	619.63
21	51.09	41.20	578.43
22	47.45	44.84	533.60
23	43.49	48.80	484.80
24	39.18	53.11	431.69
25	34.48	57.81	373.89
26	29.37	62.92	310.98
27	23.81	68.48	242.50
28	17.76	74.53	167.98
29	11.17	81.12	86.86
30	4.00	88.29	1.42

8¾% Interest

$7.87 monthly payment

Year	Interest	Principal	Balance
1	87.22	7.23	992.78
2	86.56	7.89	984.90
3	85.84	8.61	976.29
4	85.06	9.39	966.91
5	84.20	10.25	956.67
6	83.27	11.18	945.50
7	82.25	12.20	933.31
8	81.14	13.31	920.01
9	79.93	14.52	905.49
10	78.61	15.84	889.66
11	77.17	17.28	872.38
12	75.59	18.86	853.53
13	73.88	20.57	832.96
14	72.00	22.45	810.52
15	69.96	24.49	786.03
16	67.73	26.72	759.31
17	65.29	29.16	730.16
18	62.64	31.81	698.36
19	59.74	34.71	663.65
20	56.58	37.87	625.79
21	53.13	41.32	584.47
22	49.37	45.08	539.39
23	45.26	49.19	490.21
24	40.78	53.67	436.54
25	35.89	58.56	377.99
26	30.56	63.89	314.10
27	24.74	69.71	244.39
28	18.39	76.06	168.33
29	11.46	82.99	85.34
30	3.90	90.55	5.20

30 Year Term

9% Interest

$8.05 monthly payment

Year	Interest	Principal	Balance
1	89.73	6.88	993.13
2	89.08	7.53	985.60
3	88.37	8.24	977.37
4	87.60	9.01	968.37
5	86.76	9.85	958.52
6	85.83	10.78	947.75
7	84.82	11.79	935.97
8	83.72	12.89	923.08
9	82.51	14.10	908.99
10	81.19	15.42	893.57
11	79.74	16.87	876.71
12	78.16	18.45	858.26
13	76.43	20.18	838.09
14	74.54	22.07	816.02
15	72.47	24.14	791.88
16	70.20	26.41	765.48
17	67.73	28.88	736.60
18	85.02	31.59	705.01
19	62.05	34.56	670.46
20	58.81	37.80	632.67
21	55.27	41.34	591.33
22	51.39	45.22	546.11
23	47.15	49.46	496.66
24	42.51	54.10	442.56
25	37.43	59.18	383.39
26	31.88	64.73	318.67
27	25.81	70.80	247.87
28	19.17	77.44	170.44
29	11.91	84.70	85.74
30	3.96	92.65	6.90

Appendices

30
Year Term

9¼% Interest

$8.23 monthly payment

Year	Interest	Principal	Balance
1	92.23	6.54	993.47
2	91.60	7.17	986.31
3	90.91	7.86	978.46
4	90.15	8.62	969.84
5	89.32	9.45	960.40
6	88.41	10.36	950.04
7	87.41	11.36	938.69
8	86.31	12.46	926.24
9	85.11	13.66	912.59
10	83.79	14.98	897.62
11	82.35	16.42	881.20
12	80.77	18.00	863.20
13	79.03	19.74	843.46
14	77.12	21.65	821.82
15	75.03	23.74	798.09
16	72.74	26.03	772.07
17	70.23	28.54	743.53
18	67.48	31.29	712.25
19	64.46	34.31	677.94
20	61.15	37.62	640.32
21	57.51	41.26	599.07
22	53.53	45.24	553.83
23	49.17	49.60	504.24
24	44.38	54.39	449.85
25	39.13	59.64	390.21
26	33.37	65.40	324.82
27	27.06	71.71	253.12
28	20.14	78.63	174.49
29	12.55	86.22	88.28
30	4.23	94.54	6.26

9½% Interest

$8.41 monthly payment

Year	Interest	Principal	Balance
1	94.74	6.19	993.82
2	94.13	6.80	987.02
3	93.45	7.48	979.55
4	92.71	8.22	971.33
5	91.89	9.04	962.30
6	91.00	9.93	952.38
7	90.01	10.92	941.47
8	88.93	12.00	929.47
9	87.74	13.19	916.29
10	86.43	14.50	901.79
11	84.99	15.94	885.86
12	83.41	17.52	868.35
13	81.67	19.26	849.09
14	79.76	21.17	827.93
15	77.66	23.27	804.67
16	75.35	25.58	779.10
17	72.82	28.11	750.99
18	70.03	30.90	720.09
19	66.96	33.97	686.13
20	63.59	37.34	648.79
21	59.88	41.05	607.75
22	55.81	45.12	562.63
23	51.33	49.60	513.04
24	46.41	54.52	458.52
25	41.00	59.93	398.60
26	35.05	65.88	332.73
27	28.51	72.42	260.32
28	21.33	79.60	180.72
29	13.43	87.50	93.22
30	4.74	96.19	2.96

30

Year Term

9¾% Interest

$8.59 monthly payment

Year	Interest	Principal	Balance
1	97.25	5.84	994.17
2	96.65	6.44	987.74
3	96.00	7.09	980.65
4	95.28	7.81	972.84
5	94.48	8.61	964.23
6	93.60	9.49	954.75
7	92.63	10.46	944.30
8	91.57	11.52	932.78
9	90.39	12.70	920.09
10	89.10	13.99	906.10
11	87.67	15.42	890.69
12	86.10	16.99	873.71
13	84.37	18.72	854.99
14	82.46	20.63	834.37
15	80.36	22.73	811.64
16	78.04	25.05	786.60
17	75.49	27.60	759.00
18	72.67	30.42	728.58
19	69.57	33.52	695.07
20	66.15	36.94	658.14
21	62.39	40.70	617.44
22	58.24	44.85	572.59
23	53.66	49.43	523.16
24	48.62	54.47	468.70
25	43.07	60.02	408.68
26	36.95	66.14	342.55
27	30.20	72.89	269.66
28	22.77	80.32	189.35
29	14.58	88.51	100.84
30	5.55	97.54	3.31

10% Interest

$8.78 monthly payment

Year	Interest	Principal	Balance
1	99.75	5.62	994.39
2	99.16	6.21	988.19
3	98.52	6.85	981.34
4	97.80	7.57	973.78
5	97.01	8.36	965.42
6	96.13	9.24	956.18
7	95.16	10.21	945.98
8	94.10	11.27	934.71
9	92.92	12.45	922.26
10	91.61	13.76	908.51
11	90.17	15.20	893.31
12	88.58	16.79	876.53
13	86.82	18.55	857.99
14	84.88	20.49	837.50
15	82.74	22.63	814.87
16	80.37	25.00	789.88
17	77.75	27.62	762.26
18	74.86	30.51	731.75
19	71.66	33.71	698.05
20	68.13	37.24	660.82
21	64.24	41.13	619.69
22	59.93	45.44	574.25
23	55.17	50.20	524.06
24	49.91	55.46	468.61
25	44.11	61.26	407.35
26	37.69	67.68	339.68
27	30.61	74.76	264.92
28	22.78	82.59	182.34
29	14.13	91.24	91.11
30	4.58	100.79	9.68

Directory Of HUD And VA Regional Offices

HUD Regional Offices

REGION I

James J. Barry, Reg. Adm.
Rm. 800, John F. Kennedy
Federal Building
Boston, MA 02203

Area Offices

999 Asylum Avenue
Hartford, CT 06105

Bulfinch Building
15 New Chardon Street
Boston, MA 02114

Davison Building
1230 Elm Street
Manchester, NH 03101

Insuring Offices

Federal Building and Post Office
202 Harlow Street
Bangor, ME 04401

300 Post Office Annex
Providence, RI 02903

Federal Building
Elmwood Avenue
Post Office Box 989
Burlington, VT 05401

REGION II

S. William Green, Reg. Adm.
26 Federal Plaza
New York, NY 10007

Area Offices

The Parkade Building
519 Federal Street
Camden, NJ 08103

Gateway 1 Building
Raymond Plaza
Newark, NJ 07102

Grant Building
560 Main Street
Buffalo, NY 14202

666 Fifth Avenue
New York, NY 10019

Commonwealth Area Office

Post Office Box 3869 GPO
255 Ponce de Leon Avenue
Hato Rey, Puerto Rico
San Juan, PR 00936

Insuring Offices

Westgate North
30 Russell Road
Albany, NY 12206

REGION III

Theodore R. Robb, Reg. Adm.
Curtis Building
6th and Walnut Streets
Philadelphia, PA 19106

Area Offices

Universal North Building
1875 Connecticut Ave. N.W.
Washington, DC 20009

Two Hopkins Plaza
Mercantile Bank and Trust Building
Baltimore, MD 21201

Curtis Building
625 Walnut Street
Philadelphia, PA 19106

Two Allegheny Center
Pittsburgh, PA 15212

701 East Franklin Street
Richmond, VA 23219

Insuring Offices

Farmers Bank Building, 14th Floor
919 Market Street
Wilmington, VA 19801

New Federal Building
500 Quarrier Street
Post Office Box 2948
Charleston, WV 25330

REGION IV

E. Lamar Seals, Reg. Adm.
Room 211, Pershing Point Plaza
1371 Peachtree Street, N.E.
Atlanta, GA 30309

Area Offices

Daniel Building
15 South 20th Street
Birmingham, AL 35233

Peninsular Plaza
661 Riverside Avenue
Jacksonville, FL 32204

Peachtree Center Building
230 Peachtree Street, N.W.
Atlanta, GA 30303

Children's Hospital Foundation Bldg.
601 South Floyd Street
Post Office Box 1044
Louisville, KY 40201

101-C Third Floor Jackson Mall
300 Woodrow Wilson Avenue, W.
Jackson, MS 39213

2309 West Cone Boulevard
Northwest Plaza
Greensboro, NC 27408

1801 Main Street
Jefferson Square
Columbia, SC 29202

One Northshore Building
1111 Northshore Drive
Knoxville, TN 37919

Insuring Offices

3001 Ponce de Leon Boulevard
Coral Gables, FL 33134

4224-28 Henderson Boulevard
Post Office Box 18165
Tampa, FL 33679

28th Floor, 100 North Main Street
Memphis, TN 38103

U.S. Courthouse, Federal Building Annex
801 Broadway
Nashville, TN 37203

REGION V

George J. Vavoulis, Reg. Adm.
300 South Wacker Drive
Chicago, IL 60606

Area Offices

17 North Dearborn Street
Chicago, IL 60602

Willowbrook 5 Building
4720 Kingsway Drive
Indianapolis, IN 46205

5th Floor, First National Building
660 Woodward Avenue
Detroit, MI 48226

Griggs-Midway Building
1821 University Avenue
St. Paul, MN 55104

60 East Main Street
Columbus, OH 43215

744 North 4th Street
Milwaukee, WI 53203

Insuring Offices

Lincoln Tower Plaza
524 South Second Street, Room 600
Springfield, IL 62704

Northbrook Building Number II
2922 Fuller Avenue, N.E.
Grand Rapids, MI 49505

Federal Office Building
550 Main Street, Room 9009
Cincinnati, OH 45202

777 Rockwell
Cleveland, OH 44114

REGION VI

Richard L. Morgan, Reg. Adm.
Room 14C2, Earle Cabell Federal
   Building
U.S. Courthouse
1100 Commerce Street
Dallas, TX 75202

Area Offices

One Union National Plaza
Room 1490
Little Rock, AR 72201

Plaza Tower
1001 Howard Avenue
New Orleans, LA 70113

301 North Hudson Street
Oklahoma City, OK 73102

2001 Bryan Tower, 4th Floor
Dallas, TX 75201

Kallison Building
410 South Main Avenue
Post Office Box 9163
San Antonio, TX 78285

Insuring Offices

New Federal Building
500 Fannin, 6th Floor
Shreveport, LA 71120

625 Truman Street, N.E.
Albuquerque, NM 87110

1708 Utica Square
Post Office Box 52554
Tulsa, OK 74152

819 Taylor Street
Room 13A01 Federal Building
Fort Worth, TX 76102

Two Greenway Plaza East, Suite 200
Houston, TX 77046

Courthouse and Federal Office Building
1205 Texas Avenue
Post Office Box 1647
Lubbock, TX 79408

REGION VII

Elmer E. Smith, Reg. Adm.
Federal Office Building, Room 300
911 Walnut Street
Kansas City, MO 64106

Area Offices

Two Gateway Center
4th and State Streets
Kansas City, KS 66101

210 North 12th Street
St. Louis, MO 63101

Univac Building
7100 West Center Road
Omaha, NE 68106

Insuring Offices

210 Walnut Street
Room 259 Federal Building
Des Moines, IA 50309

700 Kansas Avenue
Topeka, KS 66603

REGION VIII

Robert C. Rosenheim, Reg. Adm.
Federal Building
1961 Stout Street
Denver, CO 80202

Insuring Offices

4th Floor, Title Building
909 - 17th Street
Denver, CO 80202

616 Helena Avenue
Helena, MT 59601

Federal Building
653 - 2nd Avenue N.
Post Office Box 2483
Fargo, ND 58102

119 Federal Building U.S. Courthouse
400 S. Phillips Avenue
Sioux Falls, SD 57102

125 South State Street
Post Office Box 11009
Salt Lake City, UT 84111

Federal Office Building
100 East B Street
Post Office Box 580
Casper, WY 82601

REGION IX

Robert H. Baida, Reg. Adm.
450 Golden Gate Avenue
Post Office Box 36003
San Francisco, CA 94102

Area Offices

2500 Wilshire Boulevard
Los Angeles, CA 90057

1 Embarcadero Center
Suite 1600
San Francisco, CA 94111

Insuring Offices

244 West Osborn Road
Post Office Box 13468
Phoenix, AZ 85002

801 I Street
Post Office Box 1978
Sacramento, CA 95809

110 West C. Street
Post Office Box 2648
San Diego, CA 92112

34 Civic Center Plaza
Room 614
Santa Ana, CA 92701

1000 Bishop Street, 10th Floor
Post Office Box 3377
Honolulu, HI 96813

1050 Bible Way
Post Office Box 4700
Reno, NV 89505

REGION X

James L. Young, Reg. Adm.
Arcade Plaza Building
1321 Second Avenue
Seattle, WA 98101

Area Offices

520 Southwest 6th Avenue
Portland, OR 97204

Arcade Plaza Building
1321 Second Avenue
Seattle, WA 98101

Insuring Offices

334 West 5th Avenue
Anchorage, AK 99501

331 Idaho Street
Boise, ID 83707

West 920 Riverside Avenue
Spokane, WA 99201

Appendices

VA Regional Offices

Aronov Building
474 South Court Street
Montgomery, AL 36104

3225 North Central Avenue
Phoenix, AZ 85012

Federal Office Building
700 West Capitol Avenue
Little Rock, AR 72201

Federal Building
11000 Wilshire Boulevard
West Los Angeles, CA 90024

211 Main Street
San Francisco, CA 94105

Denver Federal Center
Denver, CO 80225

450 Main Street
Hartford, CT 06103

1601 Kirkwood Highway [1]
Wilmington, DE 19805

941 North Capitol Street, NE
Washington, D.C. 20421

P.O. Box 1437
144 First Avenue, South
St. Petersburg, FL 33731

730 Peachtree Street, NE
Atlanta, GA 30308

P.O. Box 3198
680 Ala Moana Boulevard
Honolulu, HI 96801

Federal Building and U.S. Courthouse
550 West Fort Street, Box 044
Boise, ID 83724

536 S. Clark Street
P.O. Box 8136
Chicago, IL 60680

575 North Pennsylvania Street
Indianapolis, IN 46204

210 Walnut Street
Des Moines, IA 50309

5500 East Kellogg
Wichita, KS 67218

600 Federal Place
Louisville, KY 40202

701 Loyola Avenue
New Orleans, LA 70113

Togus, ME 04330

Federal Building
31 Hopkins Plaza
Baltimore, MD 21201

John Fitzgerald Kennedy
Federal Building
Government Center
Boston, MA 02203

477 Michigan Avenue
Detroit, MI 48226

Federal Building
Fort Snelling
St. Paul, MN 55111

1500 East Woodrow Wilson Ave.
Jackson, MS 39216

Room 4705 Federal Building
1520 Market Street
St. Louis, MO 63103

Fort Harrison, MT 59636

100 Centennial Mall, N.
Lincoln, NE 68508

1201 Terminal Way [2]
Reno, NV 89502

497 Silver Street
Manchester, NH 03103

20 Washington Place
Newark, NJ 07102

500 Gold Avenue, SW
Albuquerque, NM 87101

Federal Building
111 West Huron Street
Buffalo, NY 14202

252 Seventh Avenue at 24th St.
New York, NY 10001

251 N. Main Street
Winston-Salem, NC 27102

Fargo, ND 58102 [3]

Federal Office Building
1240 East Ninth Street
Cleveland, OH 44199

125 S. Main Street
Muskogee, OK 74401

1220 S.W. 3rd Avenue
Portland, OR 97204

P.O. Box 8079
5000 Wissahickon Avenue
Philadelphia, PA 19101

1000 Liberty Avenue
Pittsburgh, PA 15222

GPO Box 4867
San Juan, PR 00936

Federal Building, Kennedy Plaza [4]
Providence, RI 02903

1801 Assembly Street
Columbia, SC 29201

Courthouse Plaza Building [5]
300 N. Dakota Avenue
Sioux Falls, SD 57101

110 Ninth Avenue, South
Nashville, TN 37203

2515 Murworth Drive
Houston, TX 77054

1400 North Valley Mills Drive
Waco, TX 76710

125 South State Street
Salt Lake City, UT 84138

White River Junction, VT 05001

210 Franklin Road, S.W.
Roanoke, VA 24011

915 Second Avenue [6]
Seattle, WA 98174

502 Eighth Street
Huntington, WV 25701

342 North Water Street
Milwaukee, WI 53202

2360 East Pershing Boulevard [7]
Cheyenne, WY 82001

[1] Loan Guaranty consolidated with Philadelphia.

[2] Loan Guaranty consolidated with San Francisco. Loan Guaranty activities for Clark and Lincoln Counties, Nev. consolidated with Los Angeles.

[3] Loan Guaranty consolidated with St. Paul.

[4] Loan Guaranty consolidated with Boston.

[5] Loan Guaranty consolidated with St. Paul.

[6] Clark, Klickitat, and Skamania counties are under the jurisdiction of VARO Portland, Oregon.

[7] Loan Guaranty consolidated with Denver.

Index

when buying 94
when selling 38

B

Balloon mortgage 19, 125
Banks (see, Lending institutions)
Basement,
    finishing to upgrade property 48, 51
    insulation 54
    water leakage 87
    when selling 40
Bathrooms,
    adding 49
    remodeling 15, 52, 90
    unfinished 91
Bedrooms,
    adding 49
    number influences appeal 90
    zoning and floor plan 88
Best's Insurance Guide 112
Boom towns 78
Brick, and lower insurance rates 112
Builders,
    dealing with 71
    reputation of 64, 85
    tax deduction for 19
Building codes and permits,
    construction 71
    definition 125
    remodeling 53
Building inspector,
    and remodeling 53
    as source of information 121
Burglary insurance 111
Buyer's market,
    checklist for determining 91
    definition 126
Buying power 99
Buying real estate,
    advantages of 7
    financing 101
    from owner 82
    how to 84
    in a hurry 95, 98
    inspection checklist 87
    location 64
    negotiating 94
    risks of 8
    through broker 82
    timing 9
    to fit lifestyle 67, 88

C

Capital gains (see also, Taxes)
    avoiding by contract sale 43

A

Air conditioning,
    reducing utility costs 51
    upgrading property 51, 120
    utility company appraisal of cost 86
Amortization 125, 132
Appraisal and assessment,
    after renovation 52
    and real estate taxes 116
    assessment tax ratio 38
    as leverage 86
    before renovation 72
    before selling 73
    by utility company 86
    condominiums 120
    definitions 125
    do-it-yourself 119
    for insurance 112
    locating an appraiser 86
    methods 119
    of older homes, 92, 120
    townhouses 120
    what to ask for 86
    when buying 86
    when selling 36
Area (see, Location)
Architecture,
    brick building and insurance
        rates 112
    do-it-yourself building 71
    frame building and termites 87
    older homes, 91, 120
    renovation and remodeling 72, 73
    repair costs 76
    style should fit geographical
        region 79
Assessment (see, Appraisal and
    assessment)
Assumable mortgage 43, 125
Attic,
    insulation 59
    ventilating fans 57
Attorney (see also, Law),
    and contract sale 43
    and renting out property 27
    to serve your interests 107

avoiding by refinancing 14
avoiding by renting out property 25
definition 126
tax break for elderly 45
Caulking 56
Checklists,
    advantages of renting out property 31
    attractive features 88
    being your own broker 38
    buyer's market 91
    buying power 99
    energy saving 56, 58
    home improvement costs 51
    inspecting a house 87
    insurance 113
    lender's services 105
    livability 88
    negotiating 95
    profit when selling 45
    repairs before selling 40
    when to sell 34
    using a broker 38
Closing costs,
    avoiding 37
    definition 126
    sample form 108
Condominiums,
    advantages of 67
    appraising 120
    compared to cooperative 69, 126
    definition 126
    disadvantages of 68
    low cost of 67
    new consumer laws 67
    new vs. converted apartments 68
    renting 25, 27, 30
    storage space 90
    town houses 69, 120, 126
Construction,
    do-it-yourself building 71
    do-it-yourself improvements 67
    professional look 52
    shoddy 87
Construction industry,
    and inflation 9
    dealing with contractors 71
    effect on sales 33
    supply and demand 9
Contingency clause 35, 126
Contract sale 43
Contractors,
    dealing with 71
    definition 126
    getting questions answered 52
    insulation 57
    quality of 64
Cooperatives,
    appraising 120

Index

compared to condominiums 69
definition 126
resale 69
Credit unions,
  mortgages 104
  second mortgages 18
Custom-designing,
  counterproductive 71
  definition 126
  hard to appraise 120

D

Deferred closing date 35
Deferred tax 127
Dishwashers 58
Double-squeeze mortgage payment 35
Downpayment,
  and profit 75
  definition 127
  helping buyer obtain 41
  keep to minimum 75
  leverage 7, 101
  short vs. long-term ownership
    76, 101
  zero 101

E

Earnest money 94, 127
Elderly, tax breaks for 45
Electrical systems,
  in converted apartments 69
  main cable 88
  maintenance 85
  saving energy 58
  utility company appraisal 86
Energy saving,
  attractive to buyers 61
  checklists 56, 58
  insulation 57
Eye appeal 85

F

Fair Access to Insurance
  Requirements 112
Fans, ventilating 57, 58
Federal government (see also,
  individual agency listings and
  Taxes).
  home improvement loans 54
  tax breaks for elderly 45
  tax breaks for homeowner 8
Federal Housing Administration 127
  assumable mortgages 43
  building standards 87

guaranteed loans 8
high-ratio mortgages 76
loan when selling 41
near-zero downpayment 101
new home financing 91
vs. conventional mortgage 41
Financing (see also, Loans and
  Mortgages),
  before choosing house 101
  checklist 95
  helping buyer arrange 41
  sample form 102
  second home 30
Fire code rating 112
Fire insurance 111
Fireplace 58, 90
Floor plans,
  attractive to buyer 88
  pre-construction 64
Forms (see, Sample forms)
Frame building, and termite
  inspection 87
Furnishing 76, 95

G

Garages,
  adding 51
  reassessment 52
Garden (see, Landscaping)
Glossary of real estate terms 125
Growth areas,
  boom towns 34, 78
  locating 79

H

Heating pumps 57
Heating system,
  evaluating 87
  in converted apartments 69
  saving energy 53, 56
  when selling 40
Home improvement (see also,
  Renovation and remodeling),
  adding to resale value 9
  do-it-yourself 48, 67
  low-cost 48, 52, 72, 91
  overimproving 48
Home Owners Warranty Plan 85
Housing and Urban Development,
  Department of (HUD)
  addresses of offices 154
Humidifiers 57

I

Industry,
  and boom towns 78

lower taxes 116
office parks 79
zoning 121, 131
Inflation,
  and construction costs 9, 34, 64
  and insurance 111
  and subdivision housing 64
  how to profit from 7, 9, 14, 34
Inheritance 107
Inspecting a house 87
Insulation,
  costs 51
  finding a contractor 57
Insurance,
  checklist 113
  choosing a company 112
  choosing an agent 112
  claims 114
  fire 111
  homeowner policies 112
  ideal coverage 114
  liability 111
  mortgage life 114
  mortgage, private 31, 42, 101, 130
  needed for loan 111
  redlining 112
  types and amount of coverage 113
Interest rates,
  low for mortgages 8
  prepayment 19
  rates vs. points 101
  refinancing 15
  tables 132-153
  tax deductible 8, 14, 98, 123
Internal Revenue Service (see, Taxes)
Investment strategy,
  downpayment 75
  evaluating profit potential 85
  location 77
  prepayment of mortgage 19
  refinancing 15
  remodeling 90
  renovation 91
  renting 25
  short-vs. long-term ownership
    101, 104
  unfinished 91
  wasted asset 13

J

Joint tenancy 107, 128

K

Kitchens,
  floor plans 88

remodeling as investment 15, 90
remodeling costs 49
when selling 40

L

labor (see also, Maintenance),
do-it-yourself building 71
do-it-yourself insulation 58
low-cost 48, 52, 72, 91
professional look 52
upkeep 68, 69
landscaping,
attractive yard 9
by tenants 24
improving property 51, 67
overelaborate 48
planting a tree 51, 91
law (see also, Taxes),
building code 53, 71, 125
fire code 112
glossary of terms 125
joint tenancy 107
leases 27, 28, 129
probate 107, 130
responsibilities of landlord 24, 27
title searches 131
trust agreement 107, 128
leases, definition 129
how they work 27
sample form 28
lending institutions,
and insurance 111
avoiding double-squeeze
    payments 35
becoming a customer 98
flexibility of 101
getting information from 64, 98
in a new city 98
low mortgage rates 8
refinancing 14
renovation 53
services offered 105
setting purchase price 36
liability insurance 111
life insurance,
included in mortgage 114
to finance renovation 54
lifestyle,
and term of mortgage 104
condominium vs. single-family
    home 67
how it affects choice of home 88
loans (see also Financing and
    Mortgages),
application form 102
construction 71
renovation 53

Location,
and profit 77
boom towns 78
convenience of 77
criteria for judging 79
declining areas 65
established areas 73
fire code rating 112
importance of 63
investing in 65
new vs. older areas 78
proximity to expensive housing 48
redlining 112
rising areas 34
school district 78

M

Maintenance (see also, Repairs),
caulking 56
condominium 68
costs 68, 69, 76, 98
energy 56, 58
heating 56, 58, 87
inspecting bills 88
low-cost labor 72
town house 69
Medical facilities 77
Mortgages (see also, Financing and
    Lending institutions),
affected by repairs 92
assumable 43, 125
balloon 19, 125
creative financing 99
credit unions 104
definition 127
government-guaranteed 8
home improvements 55
insurance 31, 129
interest tables 132-153
life insurance 114
low-interest rates 8
open-end 17, 54, 129
payment in relation to salary 76
penalty clause 17
prepayment 19, 130
private 42, 101, 104, 130
rates and timing 9
refinancing 15, 16
second 15, 130
second home 30
subdivision 91
term of 104
wraparound 18, 36, 131

N

Neighborhood (see, Location)
New homes, as investment 91

O

Offer to buy 94, 96
Older building,
appraisal of 92, 120
converted apartments 68
undiscovered gems 92
Open-end mortgages 17, 54, 129

P

Penalty clause 17
Plumbing,
adding a bathroom 49
in converted apartments 69
inspecting 87
remodeling 51
septic tanks 87
water pressure 87
when selling 40
Points,
avoiding by refinancing 14
definition 130
Probate 107, 130
Profit potential (see, Investment
    strategy)
Property taxes (see, Real estate taxes)
Public transit 77, 78

R

Real estate agents and brokers,
buying in a hurry 95, 98
convenience 38
definitions of 125
determining need for 38
how to select 82
setting purchase price 36
using knowledge of 119
work for seller 94
Real estate terms, glossary of 125
Real Estate Settlement Procedure
    Act 107
Real estate taxes,
assessment 116
protesting 117
renovation reassessment 52
Record-keeping 120, 121
Records, public 123
Redlining 112
Refinancing (see also, Mortgages),
as investment 15
for business 15
for college 12, 15
profit from inflation 14
summary 20
tax savings 14

Index

Renovation and remodeling,
  choice of materials 52
  cost estimates 51, 85
  do-it-yourself 48, 67
  financing 53
  immediate profit 72
  in comparison to neighborhood
    48, 53, 72
  insurance redlining 112
  kinds to make 49
  overimproving 48
  real estate taxes 52
  tax advantages 15, 54
  timing of 53
  visible 51, 53
Rental property,
  avoiding the double-squeeze 35
  cautions 31
  for profit 24
  house vs. apartment rents 30
  managing 27
  setting rents 27
Repairs (see also, Maintenance and
    Renovation and remodeling),
  as condition of sale 92, 94
  before setting 39
  checklist 40
  energy saving 56, 58
  responsibilities of landlord 24, 27
Room size,
  attractive to buyers 90
  illusion of 40
  in converted apartments 69

S

Salary,
  and mortgage payment 76
  buying power 99
  two-income families 98
Sales contract 126
Sample forms,
  closing 108
  lease 28
  loan application 102
  offer to buy 96
Savings and loans (see, Lending
    institutions)
Schools,
  community college 77
  district 78
Second home, financing of 30
Second mortgage,
  definition 130
  for renovation 54
  how it works 18
  when selling 41
Seller's market,
  checklist 34

definition 130
Selling real estate,
  advertising 37
  do-it-yourself 37
  features checklist 88
  financing 41
  in a hurry 38
  profit checklists 34, 45
  repairs 39
  screening prospects 37
  setting purchase price 36, 42
  through broker 38
  timing 33
  using a broker checklist 38
  worksheet 40
Septic tanks 87
Shades 56, 58
Shopping centers,
  convenience of 77
  lower taxes 79, 116
  profiting from 78
  traffic 79
Single-family home,
  American dream of 67
  best investment 9
  features checklist 88
  renting 30
  selecting 74
  what to ask yourself 73
Smoke detectors 113
Solar screening 56
Soundproofing 69
Storage space 89, 90
Storm windows 51, 56
Subdivisions,
  as growth areas 62
  as rental property 31
  landscaping 91
  pre-opening prices 64

T

Taxes (see also, Real estate taxes),
  advantages of renting out property 23
  avoiding by refinancing 14
  breaks for elderly 45
  breaks for homeowner 8
  condominium dues not deductible
    25, 68
  deductions for builders 71
  deductions for repairs 39, 123
  deductions increased by
    refinancing 14
  deductions reduced by
    prepayment 19
  deferred 104, 127
  expenses reduced 98
  home improvement 123

  second mortgage 14
  wasted asset 13
  when selling 44
Tax stamps 121
Tenants,
  checking on 26
  joint 107, 128
  leases 27, 28
  property damage 24
  responsibilities to 24, 27
  suitable 26
Termite inspection 87
Title,
  and insurance claims 114
  definition 131
  retention of in contract sale 43
  search 131
Town house,
  appraisal of 120
  condominium 69
  storage space 89, 90
Traffic flow within home 90
Traffic problems 79
Trees, as an investment 51
Trust agreement 107, 128

U

Unfinished housing 91
Utility company appraisals 86

V

Veterans Administration 131,
  addresses 154
  assumable mortgage 43
  building standards 87
  downpayment 76
  guaranteed loans 8
  high-ratio loans 76
  new home financing 91
  vs. conventional mortgage 41
  when selling 41
  zero downpayment 101

W

Washing machines 58
Water heater 58
Water leakage 87
Water pressure 87
Weatherstripping 56
Wraparound mortgage 18, 36, 131

Z

Zoning,
  of community 121, 131
  of house 88